P9-CJS-938

DATE DUE

			PRINTED IN U.S.A.

The technique of Collage

Roberto Crippa   *Soleil*
Mixed Collage: a lowering sky hangs heavily over the hollow sun. The steely blues and umbers of the cork foreground are broken only by the field of newsprint

R

The technique of
Collage

HELEN HUTTON

B. T. BATSFORD LTD LONDON

WATSON-GUPTILL PUBLICATIONS NEW YORK

Riverside Community College
MAY '14 Library
4800 Magnolia Avenue
Riverside, CA 92506

N6494.C6 H8 1968
Hutton, Helen.
The technique of collage.

© Helen Hutton 1968
First published 1968
Second printing 1969
Third printing 1972
Library of Congress Catalog Card Number 68-20446

(U.K.) ISBN 0 7134 2502 4

(U.S.) ISBN 0-8230-5075-0

Printed and bound in Denmark by F. E. Bording Ltd Copenhagen
for the Publishers

B.T.BATSFORD LTD 4, Fitzhardinge Street London w.1 and

WATSON-GUPTILL PUBLICATIONS 165 West 46th Street New York NY 10036

Contents

Acknowledgment

I would like to record my very grateful thanks for the many who have helped me in the preparation of this book.

I am greatly indebted to the following for supplying me with photographs and also for help and advice in choosing these:—Mrs Kay Gimpel of Gimpel Fils, London; Mr Philip Granville of Lord's Gallery, London; Mrs Dorothy Morland of the I.C.A. Gallery, London; Mme. Benedicte Peale of Alexandre Iolas Galeris, Paris; Mr. Thomas Gibson and Mr. Gilbert Lloyd of the Marlborough Fine Art Ltd. London; and also Mr Stephen Weil of the Marlborough-Gerson Gallery, New York; Mrs Leslie Stack of the Zwemmer Gallery, London; Mrs S. Estorick of the Grosvenor Gallery, London; Dr. Henry Roland of Roland, Browse and Delbanco, London; Mlle. Ursula Schmitt, of the Sécretariat de Jean Dubuffet, Paris; Miss E. Brausen of the Hanover Gallery, London; The Schwarz Galleria, Milan, Italy; Mr Peter Cochrane of Arthur Tooth and Sons Ltd, London; Miss Marcia Bennett, of Martha Jackson Gallery, New York; Marlborough Galleria d'Arte, Rome; Miss Margareta Akermark of the Museum of Modern Art, New York.

I am especially grateful to my daughter-in-law, Marlene Hutton for German translation and to Mrs E. P. Warner for Italian translation and to Mrs Helen Gilbert of Hawaii and Mr Ray Manstrom of Cambridge for their imaginative co-operation in the schools collage experiments; to Miss Pat Douthwaite and Mr. Paul Hogarth for supplying me with endless data; and to Mr. Alan Bowness for allowing me to quote from his article on Gwyther Irwin in *Quadrum*.

And finally I want to thank Marigold Hutton for the time and patience taken with typing, my son Warwick for photography and also for designing the jacket and Mr. Sam Carr for his advice, help, and patient co-operation all the way along the line.

Introduction

Collage, from the point where we will take it up, began with the Cubists. Its invention has been individually attributed to both Picasso and Braque, whose proximity and collaboration at this time is undeniable.

Picasso's famous 'Still Life with Chair Caning' united oil paint with pasted-on oil cloth, while the first *papiers collés* were undoubtedly done by Braque. As a technique of picture-making, the term 'collage' comes from the French verb *coller* to paste, stick, glue; and *papier collé* is the more restricted expression referring only to paper.

Collage itself is now an accepted art form, making a direct contribution towards creative expression; unrestricted by difficult techniques, each artist has discovered his own approach through the character of his medium. The image-making urge which has been latent in man since primitive times finds spontaneous manifestation in collage-making. As several artists have admitted in their commentaries, it was the only way out of an impasse that they had reached at some difficult stage of artistic expression and it has brought, to them, a new liberation of vision and form.

The Dada movement, which flourished in Europe from 1915 until 1923, was a cult of anti-art and was an important development in the collage concept, relating it through symbolism to the changing social scene. This period saw the emergence of two major artists in the medium: Max Ernst (whose work may be seen in all the important galleries) and Kurt Schwitters. Ernst either invented or developed most of the known technical methods, often transcribing them from earlier ones. Kurt Schwitters, whose now famous statement 'the waste of the world becomes my art', found his medium in the fragmented rubbish on the streets and in dustbins, and from this produced collages that in their range of methods, styles and forms have enriched the world of art ever since.

The Surrealists also made their contribution. André Breton, who was the mouthpiece for the movement, stated in the First Manifesto of Surrealism issued in 1924 that it was 'purely psychic automatism'. Their goal was no longer anti-art, but an expression of the artist's psyche by recording the hitherto unfathomable depths of the unconscious as symbolised by dreams.

This aim was achieved in their collages and paintings by the juxtaposition of objects and ideas, the aim being to achieve surprise and even horror, through illogicality; embracing ethics and politics in their art. Predominant in this movement were such artists as Salvador Dali, Max Ernst, Joan Miró and René Magritte, all of course names of international stature.

Techniques springing from this movement include *'Frottage'*, *'Décalcomanie'*, 'Photomontage' and 'Photogram'. These are described in detail in the relevant sections.

The value of collage as a means of developing expression in an art form has been widely recognised by art schools. In the field of design and spatial relationship, a revaluation may be made as the work progresses and infinite variations considered. The presentation here of the working methods and formative approach of this selection of artists engaged in this medium, may stimulate an awareness of the validity of collage as an art form and a recognition of the significance inherent in everyday materials.

As the term 'collage' is a canopy extending over a wide area which includes assemblage, construction in depth and even possibly 'environ-mental happenings', it has been found necessary to limit the scope of this book to works on a two-dimensional plane (with a very few exceptions, generally where the focus on originality of technique justified the inclusion.) A few examples of assemblage, notably Schwitters and Dubuffet are, however, shown.

Further it must be emphasized that if the choice of artists selected and quoted appears to be arbitrary, the primary intention is that the book should offer examples of different approaches and techniques, not only by artists of international importance, who may be seen in galleries, both public and art dealers', but of others who have explored different aspects of this medium and perhaps made new enrichment.

In a general way the artists have been grouped under the techniques applicable to their work, but as the majority of collage artists combine several media and widely differing technical approaches, this grouping must necessarily seem capricious and many of the major artists have been included in an individual section.

Two experimental collage projects have been worked out specially in art schools for inclusion here. One was done in the U.S.A. at the University of Hawaii, where the majority of students are of oriental origin and the feeling for tonal quality and space projects its image.

The same project was shown to young students at Impington Village College in Cambridge. Although originating along similar lines, the results, under different background, attitude and direction, present a completely divergent vision. Both may be thought equally interesting, not least because of the contrast in their results.

Part one TECHNIQUES

This section is intended to cover many of the techniques involved in collage and some of the media used. 'Technique' in the sense of skill of execution is only thinly applicable to collage, in the sense that the individual artist in his creative pursuit of his problem, instinctively determines his material, and his approach to a technique is resolved by its identity. Some examples of the work of individual artists are given with brief comments.

The basis of most collage and indeed, the classic medium, is paper: paper in its many guises, forms and moods, evoking nostalgic imagery (old labels, tickets, postcards, letters, dead cheques and faded photographs), all jealously defending their identities and analogies. Peeled off and torn posters, thrown-away papers, creased and tattered newsprint and wrapping paper are all eloquent presences of a saddened, transient fragility. Paper is mutely vulnerable, faded, torn and burnt, dissolving and changing character in water from crisp finite forms to a fluid amorphic medium. Its versatility of character is only limited or extended by the imagination of the artist who handles it.

Selection and disposition express in terms of design, the mood and character of the artist. Torn, cut, moulded wet, burnt, scorched—each type of edge utters an individual sound, reflecting serenity, sadness, anger or humour. It has qualities of opacity that draw down a blind on the image, arousing illusory forms such as those found in Oriental art.

The delicately textured papers from Japan, bearing such names as Kinwashi, Shogi, Sakawa, Mingei, and Teng Jo to mention but a few, conjure up visions of mists, mountains and waters that float across the early Oriental screens.

Hard-cut edges of paper and card as shown in the examples of Severini, Barbara Engle and John Christopherson, state logical reality, assert thickness and solidity. Precise shaping, cutting and placing dictate these techniques.

Many others have evolved fortuitously, such as the laminations of cloth or papers, as in the case of Marca-Relli, who works with intense speed, building up one shape on top of another, or Gwyther Irwin, whose torn posters develop into the vehicle of expression for his ideas on rock formation and rhythm of the sea. Tearable and peelable media have originated techniques of scraping, peeling away and burning.

Paper is softened and made malleable with water, glues and acrylic mediums; large sheets are tinted in colour baths (inks, water colour or diluted oil colour), torn and cut into designed or random shapes, placed directly on to prepared or painted base, or stuck down experimentally, leaving edges lapped free. Motherwell's technique is interesting in this respect. Many artists store away an unlimited supply of tinted torn shapes as a painter stores his paints.

Many leading artists of our time have carried out their experiments in mixed media, over-painting or drawing over the paper sections, or covering glue-spread areas with soil or sand. Picasso has used sawdust and Dubuffet used earth, coal, pebbles, dried plants and leaves. Schwitters has combined every possible element, usually gathered from the garbage can, the pavement and rubbish of all sorts.

Assemblage

The action of collecting and assembling media, usually on a three-dimensional plane in collage form may be termed 'assemblage.' Constructions of welded metal, glued wood sections, found objects and discarded fragments of remote relationship or diverse imagery occupy this field and works of three artists, outstanding in all collage techniques and media are shown; Schwitter's Merz assemblages, Dubuffet's assemblages and Burri's welded metal construction assemblages.

A 'Found' Collage: this was discovered on the wall of an old pub and is a fine example of formal placing and selection in the rich variation of the lettering

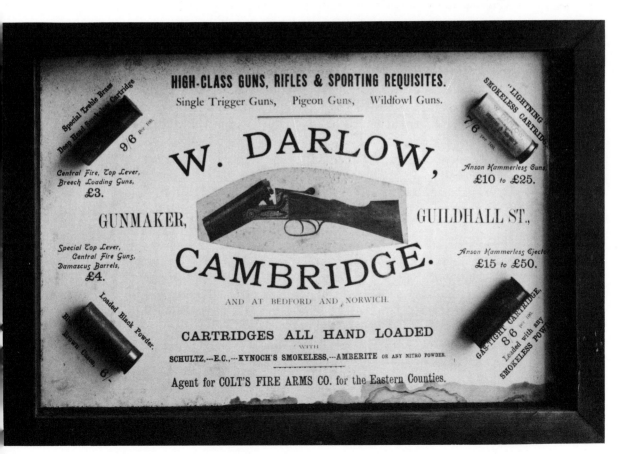

Kurt Schwitters occupies a unique position as having been one of the out-standing collage artists of our time, in addition to being a painter, sculptor and poet of considerable stature. Most of the techniques, approaches and discovered media were either invented, extended or prophesied by him during the period that he worked in this medium, which was from 1914, through the period of Dada (1917-1924) until his death in comparative obscurity in England in 1948.

Although for most of his life Schwitters was compelled to earn his living as an academic portrait painter, he found his true medium as early as 1914 in scrap paper and rubbish gathered from pavements, dust bins, the litter of towns and cities. As he wrote in a foreword to his 1920 exhibition 'Merz': 'Every artist must be allowed to mould a picture out of nothing but blotting paper, for example, providing he is capable of moulding a picture.' (From *Dada Painters and Poets,* edited by Robert Motherwell, published by Witten-born, Schultz Inc. New York, 1951).

In actual scale his work was diminutive, many collages being as small as a postcard, but the range of his palette—his media—was infinite. Everything that had been discarded and thrown away he loved and treasured: tram tickets, stamps, envelopes, shoe soles and laces, string, newspaper, bills, numbers and letters, wood shavings, photographs, feathers, torn rags and sacks, shredded, holed and battered.

The term 'Merz' was coined by Schwitters for his collage pictures. He has described the origin of the expression thus: 'I gave to my new manner of work, based on the use of these materials, the name Merz. This is the second syllable of the word Kommerz. This name was born out of one of my pictures; an image on which one reads the word Merz cut out of the Kommerz und Privatbank advertisement and stuck among abstract shapes—when for the first time I exhibited these images made of paper, glue, nails, etc.... I had to find a generic name to designate these new species...Therefore I called all my pictures...Merz pictures, the name of the most characteristic one...' (from *Dada Painters and Poets,* as above).

Merz not only included the hundreds of small collages made by Schwitters during his prolific lifetime, but about 20 large ones and three Merz architectural constructions, the first of which, the Merzbau, was built in Hanover, his home town, and called The Column or The Cathedral of Erotic Misery. It was an abstract three-dimensional collage made of cardboard, wood, iron, broken furniture—grotto-like in the strangely moulded plaster caverns hidden in the rambling sculpture which contained secret doors, opening only to the initiated.

This Merzbau was destroyed by bombing in 1943 after Schwitters had fled from Nazi Germany, and he built a second one in Norway. This also was

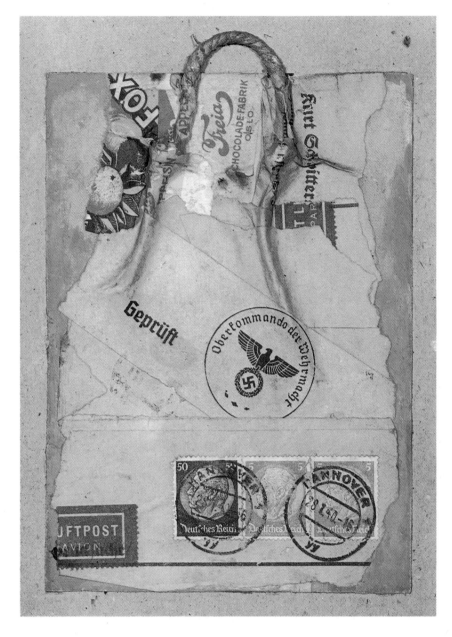

Kurt Schwitters *Geprüft*
Collage Assemblage: the evocative and haunting colour
sequence of this formal collage statement bring it into line
with the most significant of Schwitters work

urt Schwitters *Merzbild 29 mit Drehrad*
erz Assemblage: one of Schwitters early and contro-
rsial Merz pictures, bits and pieces from the refuse and
ins of World War I, fitted into a combination assem-
age and thus creating new art values

destroyed, by fire in 1951. His final Merzbau, which he now called Merzbarn, as it was built in a barn at Ambleside, England, was never completed as by this time he was in poor health. He died here in 1948, aged 60. The single wall which he finished has been preserved by the farmer, named Pierce, who lent him the barn, and in 1965 it was removed to Newcastle by the Fine Arts Department of the University of Newcastle.

Most of the techniques mentioned in this book have been explored by Schwitters. An interesting observation on one of his working methods is made by Charlotte Weidler (and quoted in *Collage* by Harriet Janis and Rudi Blesh, Chilton Co. Publishers, Philadelphia and New York, 1962): 'He spread flour and water over the paper, then moved and shuffled and manipulated his scraps of paper around in the paste while the paper was wet. With his finger tips he worked little pieces of crumbled paper into the wet surface; also spread tints of water colour or gouache around to get variations in shadings of tone. In this way he used flour both as a paste and as a paint. Finally he removed the excess paint with a damp rag, leaving some like an overglaze in places where he wanted to veil or mute a part of the colour.'

This was but one of his many approaches to collage and only a careful examination of his works will disclose his creative use of improbable media.

One of his most important contributions to art, indeed, to all human interest, lies in his ability to evoke an awareness of the presence of natural collage in the life around us; in the street, the bus, on wharves, wall and derelict buildings; wet by rain and blown by winds, discarded fragments are the richesse of his world—and ours.

Kurt Schwitters *Basket Ring*
Relief Collage: in this relief collage of Schwitters the basket ring is on wood base.

Kurt Schwitters *Teeth* (left)
Merz Relief: a Merz relief that becomes a sculptured image in its simple formal statement

Kurt Schwitters *Merzbild 46a Das Kegelbild Merz* Assemblage: a Merzbild or collage-assemblage showing the inter-relationship of grouped simple objects

Kurt Schwitters *Heavy Relief* Relief Assemblage: in this assemblage in heavy relief, the projection of the various forms is considerable and the work on a larger scale than is usual for Schwitters

Alberto Burri   *Grande Ferro*
Metal Collage: an example of the 'Ferri' of 1958-1959 when
scrap metal, iron and steel are assembled into formal areas,
usually with the gaping wound healed by welding the metal
sheets together

Roberto Crippa *Oiseau* (right)
Wood Collage: this collage of pitted and riven driftwood is
a projection of strongly opposed forms using media in a
starkly raw state

Roberto Crippa *Person*
Wood Collage: the Person stands against the dark barricade
in this collage, rigid, in stark wood and carved cork

MAX ERNST

Collage as defined by Ernst is the explorations of 'the fortuitous encounter upon a non-suitable plane of two mutually distant realities'. ('Beyond Painting', by Max Ernst in *Cahiers d' Art,* 1937).

    In stature he is one of the most distinguished artists of our time and his art embraces a great range of inherent contradictions; formal abstractions to minute segments of realism.

    An intellectual, with deep reservoirs of philosophy and learning, his

Max Ernst *Loplop présente une jeune fille*
Montage—Collage: Ernst's recurring ima[ge]
of 'Loplop, the Superior of Birds', the ph[an]
tom which haunted him from early chi[ld]
hood finds expression in this monta[ge.]
Arising out from a textured backgrou[nd]
a series of haunting media is assemb[led]
beneath Loplop

classical education becomes apparent in his many literary allusions and witticisms. These found expression in his writings and collages during the period of Surrealism and Dada.

When only six years old he had his first contact with the forces of death and destruction, when his sister, having kissed him goodbye, died a few hours later. Visions and the fear of death began to pursue him and through all of his later work lies this thread of a menacing evil, lurking beneath the surface.

In his early teens he was confronted with the sight of a dead bird, a devoted pet. At this moment he was told of the birth of his sister Lori, and this further confrontation with life and death caused a series of emotional upheavals, resulting in a neurosis connecting birds and humans. This weaves a way thematically through much of his work—his identification with Loplop, the Superior of the Birds. (A collage of this chimera is reproduced.)

Against this emotional background his imaginative approach to art was conceived and most of his technical exploration was a direct result of some personal experience. While staring at floorboards, he became fascinated with the patterns, and placing paper over them, rubbed through an impression of the wood grain with soft pencil. The resulting *frottage* formed the basis for his imprint collage technique.

His print collages were gleaned from old engravings and prints from many sources; medical journals, engineering journals, advertisements, scientific illustrations, Victorian steel-engravings; the strange juxtaposition of this imagery produced psychological overtones and haunting nostalgia. His now famous book *La Femme 100 Têtes* was a remarkable example of this collage technique, narrating in 149 sequences his fantasia of Loplop.

Décalcomanie was also developed by Ernst, in the creation of further imagery in the chance configurations produced by this technique. Variations on *grattage* attracted his attention and by texturing wet paint with such tools as forks, rulers, knives, he produced visionary shapes.

Déchirage, découpage, papier collé and photomontage may all be found in the strange Gothic world akin to the Germanic Middle Ages, seeking expression through the art of Max Ernst.

Gravure and Lithographic Assemblage This technique was primarily exploited by Max Ernst; the media was basically old engravings assembled to produce a fantastic and improbable imagery in collage form. The *Femme 100 Têtes* of which he did many variations is a well-known example.

Max Ernst   *La Paix, La Guerre et la Rose*
Collage on Plywood: the satirical poignant comment on peace, war and the rose is expressed here in Ernst's own terms. The paint-smeared palette represents peace perhaps, the general behind the golden grid (Loplop again?) and the torn virginity of the rose petal

Max Ernst   *Laïcité*
Collage Assemblage: the assembled forms here also bring their message '*Ne pas confondre le baiser de la fée avec la fessée de l'abbé*'. The subtly placed forms identified with pagan temples; the slap from the abbot. This is one of a series of Ernst's latest collage experiments

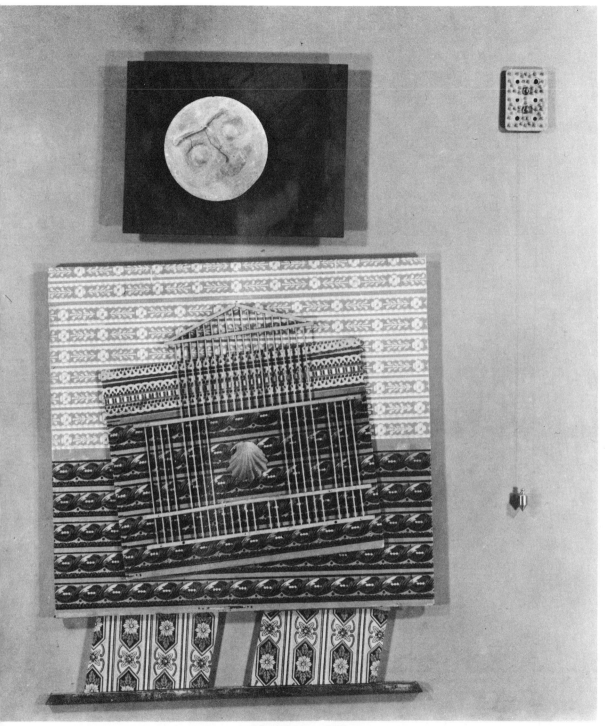

Max Ernst   *Soliloque*
Collage on Plywood: a royal blue sun rises through a darkly
red shaded screen on a laquer red background; the wall-
papered rectangles which dominate the centre form an
opposing grid to the pagan temple. The scallop shell of the
Botticelli Venus floats within

Max Ernst   *Maison en Feu et Ange en Tablier Blanc*
Collage on Plywood: against a deep purple, a temple is
burning, watched over by the angel of the white tablecloth.
This form in cut-out lace is attached to a dark board which
is in slight projection

Max Ernst *Première Pensée*
Collage on Plywood: on a fern-shadowed backcloth, the
sun rises over a blood-red sky as seen through a porthole.
The bird chimera again presents its haunting image in front
of the open shutters

Although Dubuffet has not accepted the term 'collage' as applicable to his work, and has preferred to call it *assemblage,* his contribution to this approach, whatever the terminology, is of outstanding value. His explorations have ranged over an infinite field of subjects, media and techniques, all of which are bent to express his basic philosophy, first manifested in his exhibition in Paris in 1946. The works shown presented such violence and disturbing imagery as to cause shock and uproar in its withdrawal from all hitherto accepted art values. Called *'l'art brut',* it was considered to be something beyond nature in the raw.

He stated during a lecture to the Arts Club of Chicago in 1951: 'Personally I believe very much in the values of savagery. I mean instinct, passion, mood, violence, madness. I want to begin by telling you how my conception (of beauty) differs from the usual one. The latter believes that there are beautiful objects and ugly objects... Not I. I believe that beauty is nowhere. I consider this notion of beauty as completely false... I think that the Greeks are the ones to first purport that certain objects are more beautiful than others... It is distressing to think of people deprived of beauty because they do not have a straight nose or are too corpulent or old.'

He further justifies his philosophy in a statement made by him and quoted from the catalogue of the retrospective Dubuffet exhibition in the Musée des Arts Decoratifs, Paris, 1961: 'I have always loved—it is a sort of vice—to employ only the most common materials in my work, those that one does not dream of at first because they are too crude and close at hand and seem unsuitable for anything whatsoever. I like to proclaim that my art is an enterprise to rehabilitate discredited values.'

In this mood he explored many techniques which found expression in strange mediums. By glueing, cementing, spattering, pasting, printing, painting, texturing sgraffito (to produce his *texturologies* and *topographies*) he requisitioned such materials as clinker, sand, earth, sponges, stones, butterfly wings, newspaper torn or crumpled. The range of botanical elements included agave, banana peel, artichoke, orange peel, plane leaf, mullein, burdock, fig, carrot flowers and calyx, cabbage, rhubarb, spinach beet, lotus, magnolia, tangerine peel, bean shells, pumpkin, paulownia, convolvulus, ivy and hart's tongue. The assemblages composed of these were known as 'Éléments Botaniques' and represented figures or landscape or figures in landscape, constructed from a humus-like accretion, pastoral and elemental in substance.

Jean Dubuffet   *L'Offreur de Bouquet*
Gravure Assemblage: this collage is an example of a gravure assemblage; the lithographs used being printed from ink-spattered textures, finally cut and glued. The figure formed is man destroyed as a myth; rather an integration of his surroundings

His *Assemblages d'Empreintes* consisted of lithographs made by pasting pieces of cut transfer paper (previously textured and spattered by lithographic ink) to stone for printing.

The *Tableaux d'Assemblages* were a combination of oil and assembled media, butterfly wings, cut lithographs etc., into the well-known collage pictures. His *Concretions Terreuses* were paintings of earth and pavement, thick laminations of dried leaves, flowers etc., assembled onto canvas.

Several of his *Éléments Botaniques* are illustrated here in addition to the *Assemblages d'Empreintes* lithographs, *Tableaux d'Assemblages* and *Assemblages Papiers*.

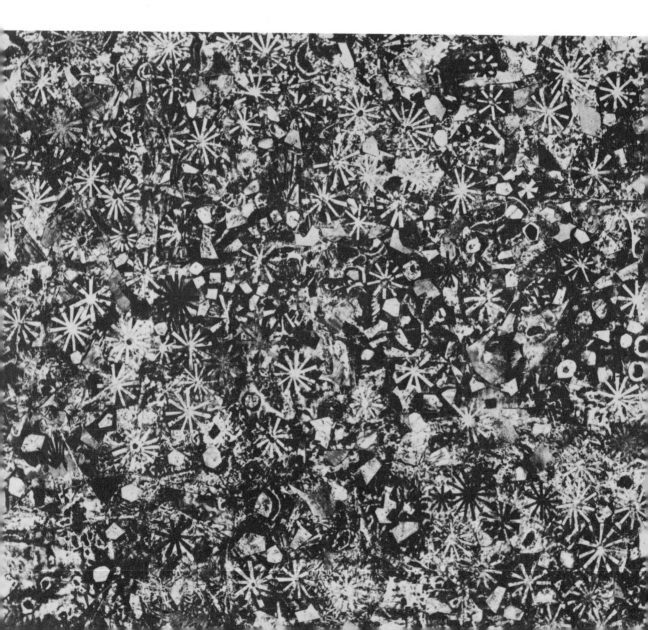

Jean Dubuffet *Le Gason* (left)
Assemblage Picture: the elements here are
botanical to the extent of being herbaceous.
The sensuous quintessence of earthiness,
flowers and grass emanates from this collage

Jean Dubuffet *Les Faits s'eteignent d'autres
s'allument*
Assemblage: a brilliant pattern assemblage
in which the elements are various media,
ink, gouache, imprints and probably pen-
scratchings and brush drawings on saturated
paper

Jean Dubuffet   *Feuillage à l'Oiseau*
Lithographic Assemblage: the 'Bird in the Tree' is a further
example of lithographic assemblage, but here the forms are
drawn in careful delineation of their identities. The bird
perches sadly on a tree of skeleton leaves

Jean Dubuffet *Implantations*
Texturologie Peinture Collage: the objects in this assemblage
have shed their personality to merge and become a rich pastoral, the sharply defined forms sacrificing their identities to the
final statement. '*Implantations*' expresses Dubuffet's strong
feeling for the elementals of nature in the image of geological and plant life. The technique combines the cut and pasted
sections with the vivid blue painted horizon

Jean Dubuffet *Halte et Répit*
Gravure Assemblage: this gravure assemblage is a collage
of strongly conceived and composed units. The various
textured areas in saturated ink, spattering, scratching,
décalcomanie, and possibly wax-resist, all make their contribution towards the acceptance of Man

Kenneth Rowntree *Glass Collage*
Kenneth Rowntree's collage assemblages in glass and other
media show how a group of objects are changed and unified
when seen through the layers of tinted glass. The heighten-
ing of visual values is achieved by the insertion of bands
of coloured glass or the whiteness of the painted wood at
the edges

Alberto Burri *Combustione* (detail)
Collage Combustioni: this *combustione* is fairly
typical of the collages in burned wood,
the charred edges and holes burned with a
blowlamp (blowtorch) and then fitted together again in a manner suggestive of
jointed bones

Fumage

The formation of tones over sectional areas is made by passing a tongue
of smoke from a candle or smouldering wick over the dampened surface of
the collage. Cloth may be smoked similarly, wet or dry, and later applied in
sections to the collage surface.

This is allied to the burning technique and may be done on a dry base,
but the resulting shapes are made by the smoke, as the flame is removed before carbonization takes place.

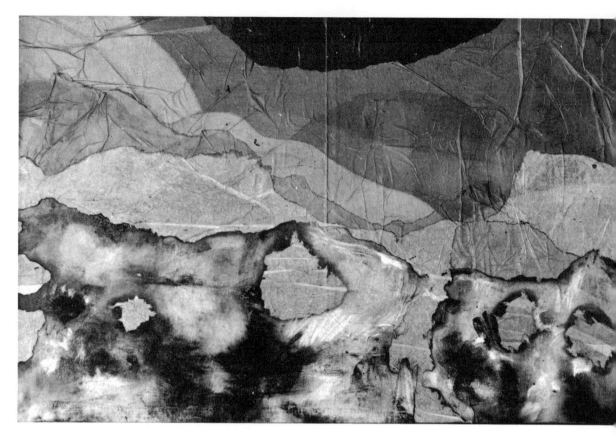

Student Work
Brûlage—Fumage: the rags seen in the foreground were
damped and then perforated by burning holes with the
flame of a candle. The darker areas were subjected to the
smoke only

Brûlage

For *Brûlage* the paper (this also applies to fabric) is burned in any way that
suggests itself to the artist, by being passed over a candle flame or lamp where
certain areas are scorched or burnt, an action easier to carry out if the paper
is rather damp so that the size and shape of the burnt area may be controlled.
Sometimes the material may be burned before being used in the collage, and
the carbonised edges left to outline shapes and apertures. Burri ignites the
paper, and while it is alight allows it to fall onto a prepared plaster ground,
finding fortuitous forms. This is later fixed with transparent vinyl medium.
These collages are known as *'combustioni'*.

Detail of *Brûlage—Fumage:* the creased rags in the fore-ground are crunched up for burning and have not yet been flattened and pasted down. A strangely Oriental landscape is emerging

Découpage

The delineation of a clearly conceived line is usually carried out with scissors, razor blade or sharp cutting edge. This was the original method of the hard-edge school and has a strong influence on this type of painting. Rather substantial paper or card is used and this is sometimes stained or painted before cutting. Two methods of colouring the paper used for collage are mentioned here.

Winnifred Hudson uses finest quality watercolour and lays the sheets in baths of this, drying them, either by laying them flat on sheets of glass or pegged up on a line like washing.

Ben Norris works with mixed stains, sometimes combining water colour with acrylic, taking advantage of the chemical reaction of these opposing media to arrive at surprising textures. He keeps a vast 'palette' of these coloured papers.

Artists working the technique of *Découpage* include Severini, Antonio Saura (cut-out forms over-worked with gouache), John Christopherson and Barbara Engle (cut forms of thin cardboard).

John Christopherson   *Sea-Tower and Moon*
Découpage: the collage was built with several layers of pape which had been deliberately faded by leaving in the ope air. Semi-transparent tissue paper was also used in such a wa that the under layers showed through. The black of the sk was painted in afterwards and part of the paper allowe to show beneath

39

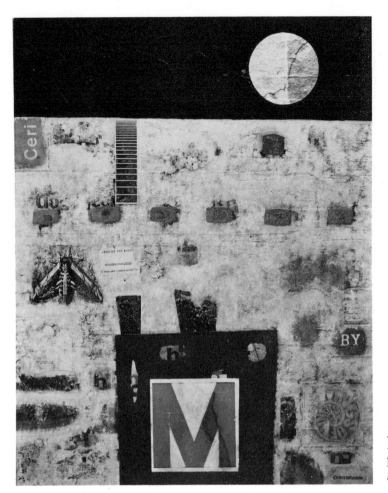

John Christopherson *Fortress 'M'*
Découpage: the sky in black lacquer over
paper which is briefly apparent. Moon
gold Japanese wall-paper

JOHN CHRISTOPHERSON

Christopherson says: 'I was first attracted to this medium by its rather poetic
nature and by the fact that it transforms various disparate materials that would
otherwise have been dispersed.

I usually start a collage with a general idea of the design and bring together
the various pieces of paper which will be appropriate to this. Each collage
is composed of several layers with those beneath showing through, which
is similar to the glaze technique that I use in oil painting.

The paper used may be prints, handprinted wallpaper, exhibition cards,
sweet wrappings, tissue papers. I often leave these latter out of doors for some
time to weather and fade, but I do feel that it is a mistake to use poor quality
paper such as newsprint, as this soon results in excessive fading and 'brown-
ing', as may be seen in some of the early French collages. The glue used is
'Polycell'. An American Equivalent would be Elmer's Glue.

John Christopherson *Landscape with Greek Column*
Découpage: paper Collage. Archaeological motif dominated
by Greek column and remains. The landscape is mainly
black and white with multi-coloured areas of pink, orange,
violet and blue. Sky of light and dark violet tissue paper
with photographic background showing through. Gold
moon of Japanese paper

Barbara Engle   *White on White*
Découpage: Drawing Paper, Watercolour Paper, Japanese
Rice Papers, (heavy quality with fibres, some thin patterned)
cut pieces of cork. Glued with polymer acrylic and painted
white. Basic colour scheme is white with some greyish overtones and some yellowish. Colour variations coming from
the varieties of papers used

White on White   (detail)

Gino Severini *Still Life*
Découpage: the work of Severini presents a classic example of
Découpage, the hard edge, cut and sharply delineated in shape,
often combined with other material such as corrugated
cardboard, playing cards, tickets, metallic foil, with areas
drawn over with crayon or over-painted with oil. In some of
his earlier work during the Cubist period he introduced such
things as sequins and similar frivolities. The example shown
is fairly typical of his work

Austin Cooper *Abstraction 199/62*
Affiches Lacerés: his medium is a combination of water-colour, scraps of paper and paste, kneaded and moulded into an impasto from which the collage emerges

Affiches Lacerés

This may hardly be classified as a technique, but rather an idea of using discarded material (in the form of hoardings, old posters, notices, etc.) which tended to develop into a technique in its own right. Several artists have worked in this medium, finding in the colourful stripped fragments the muted under-tones of the people; a genre art of today.

Some work in a non-associative way, tearing and over-laying uniformly sized sections until the original identity of the paper is lost. Gwyther Irwin accumulates quantities of old posters ripped from the hoardings, but uses only the reverse side so that the colour is monochromatic and any lettering fades into anonymity.

Austin Cooper has been called a 'tachiste' and in denying it he suggests that his random placing of found paper stems from the unconscious. Other artists have deliberately presented expressive sections, with their evocative messages of travel, cruises, food, drink, film announcements, patent medicines—events and objects which have vanished into the past, penetrating the paper mask.

Austin Cooper *Tal-lee*
Paper Collage: The amorphous forms float across a space
that is limitless. A sculptural, paper collage

AUSTIN COOPER

His technique is basically that of *décollage* and *affiches lacerés,* the glueing,
moulding and tearing off of scraps of waste paper. The paper and paste is
mixed with water colour pigment and worked into an impasto, and although
having something in common with Schwitters in his treatment of these
materials, his design is less formal and disciplined and has no definite axis,
horizontal or vertical. He leaves the interpretation to the perception of the
onlooker; rejecting conscious design, he allows his fingers to do as they will
with the paper scraps and the final result is fortuitous, although a certain
conscious selection probably operates in his choice of colour.

GWYTHER IRWIN

He has insisted that his work is a sequence of experiences that flow from the
visual impact of the rock-textured coastline of Cornwall.
    Alan Bowness writing in *Quadrum* says, in discussing Irwin's technique:—
    'The early collages were mainly of two kinds—a dense build-up of small

46

scraps of used papers, completely covering the surface, (as in 'Albino' 1963) or, like 'Collage No. 6', a torn and lacerated parchment-like sheet, (always the back of a poster) mounted like a shield on a dark ground … A misty, mysterious, threatening air hangs over some of these works; others hint at a moment of enlightenment. The textural interest is always strong, tonal variation is subtle and refined, inviting close-up contemplation.

'By 1961 the dense all-over quality of most of the earlier work had given way to a more frank acceptance of the dichotomy between surface and glued paper: more light and air had come into the work and a new and clean-cut openness became its main characteristic. 'Bauxite Baby' (detail shown) represents this new and perhaps definitive phase of the paper collage. Texture is still important, but Irwin's interest in the collage material for its own sake is now (and remains) minimal. Strips of torn paper are pasted down on a black or white ground, and suddenly, the voids become more significant than the solid forms. To explore this, Irwin changes his medium and begins using lengths of string, in themselves of constant size, glued at varying intervals onto the surface ('Cord on Bleu' 1961), which is dominated by rhythmic movements strongly suggestive of wave and water patterns.

'There is already a certain relief element in the string, and this has become more pronounced in Irwin's most recent medium—matt black cardboard cut into strips and mounted edgeways, on a board or in a shallow box. The projecting edge is sometimes split with a fingernail ('Phantom'), and the general effect is one of mysterious stratification, as reminiscent of certain geological formations as the string collages are of wave movements.'

Gwyther Irwin himself has commented on his approach to collage, as follows:—

'In 1957 when I made my first collage. I was concerned with simple, large, slab-like forms which, coincidentally, were very like the shapes offered by the thick mass of battered, weathered posters which were either torn off or fell off, outside poster hoardings.

'The colour of the back of these posters (I never used the front), sometimes milky and subdued, sometimes ginger and rusty where they had been in contact with iron, was also the type of colour that I was already using, and so the paper was a logical, almost inevitable step.

'My source of material did not remain exclusively posters from hoardings; various ideas claimed my attention so that different materials were needed to express them. This is most important, as it is often assumed, quite erroneously that materials can be used for their own sake.

'My working technique is always the same—very slow and arduous. It consists of glueing hundreds of similar elements together and across a surface…attempting rigorous control/selection of each individual act of pairing, while, at the same time, hoping that one day my conscious mind will really stop interfering with and dictating the over-all shape. I always work from one side of the surface across to the other side because I do not wish to provide visual stepping stones, which, in my case, are a sort of false security. I use a very closed technique and work in a very open situation, the collage elements providing the closed technique.

'My only general view on collage is that I cannot really consider it in isolation or as an offshoot of painting. The important thing is whether the work is meaningful; the material matters not one jot.

'One cannot have something that is good only *because* it is made of a certain material—it is there and it works; but one can have something that is bad because it is made of a certain material. This, perhaps, is the danger inherent in the medium. But when used as a tool for one's conceptualization, it can release directions which would otherwise not have occurred.'

Gwyther Irwin *Bauxite Baby*
Affiches Lacerés: a typical Irwin collage of strips of torn paper (backings from old posters) pasted on a black ground, the negative dark areas assuming more importance than the solid foreground forms

Winnifred Hudson *Arabian*
Déchirage: 'Arabian' is a series of coloured shapes, of opaque
Japanese ricepaper, put together with wheatpaste; not
saturated, but applied from the back of the piece, and assembled in such a way as to give a general feeling of landscape
space

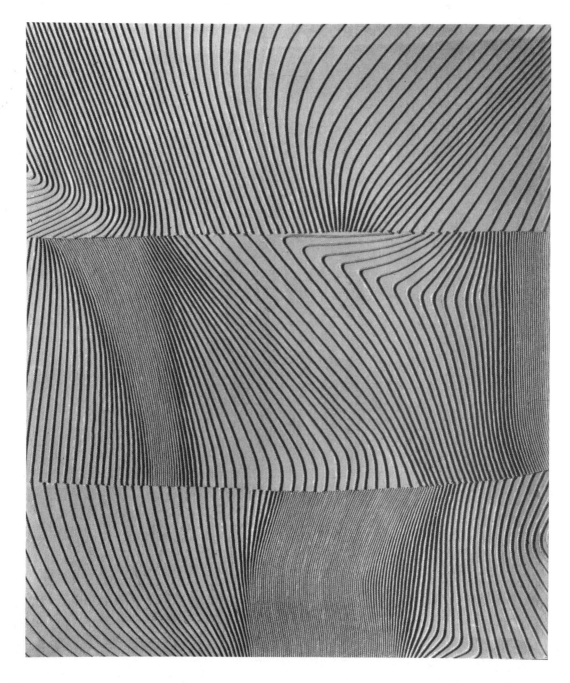

Gwyther Irwin *Cord on Bleu*
String Collage: this is a collage in which the interest is centered on optical phenomena. In each of the three string sections, a rippling pattern moves across the surface, reminiscent of the moods and rhythms of the sea

yther Irwin   *Collage No 6*
iches Lacerés: in this collage the structure and texture of
k formation is strongly evoked in the torn and crumbling
lity of this discarded poster backing

Gwyther Irwin   *Albino*
Affiches Lacerés: a further example of the more ordered
affiches lacerés technique, again using the backs of posters but
where more density of surface covering is a feature

Déchirage

The haphazard quality of the torn edge of paper possesses a unique flexibility and expressiveness. It may be moved, layered, transposed, breaking free from rigid discipline to allow free forms to emerge. It combines weight with weightlessness, thickness with transparency, making spatial statements with a clarity that contradicts its subtle overtones. Softened with water or glue, it is transformed into a plastic medium that may be creased and crinkled, modelled and twisted until it is as malleable as oil paint.

The Japanese rice papers lend themselves perfectly to tearing and are far more widely used in the U.S.A. than in Europe. John Kjargaard, a Danish artist working in Hawaii, works with them and produces a very sensitive alliance of the Orient with the sensuous vegetation of the Pacific. Other examples of *Déchirage* are found in the work of Motherwell, Barbara Engle and Winnifred Hudson.

The paper is wetted either with glue or water, by brushing over with the liquid or by soaking it. It may be moulded or twisted into the shapes or areas dictated by the design, often over-laying several tones of the same colour. Most artists combine this with other methods of using paper or with other media.

ROBERT MOTHERWELL

He has worked in Papier Collé or a combination of paper and painting for the past twenty odd years and must be regarded as one of the leading artists in this field. His delineated shapes speak with great spatial clarity and the statement is always resolved with directness and brevity.

He wrote the following comment in an article 'Beyond the Aesthetic' (DESIGN Vol 47 No. 8, April 1946):—

'The sensation of physically operating on the world is very strong in the medium of the papier collé collage, in which various kinds of paper are pasted to the canvas. One cuts and chooses and shifts and pastes, and sometimes tears off and begins again. In any case, shaping and arranging such a relational structure obliterates the need, and often the awareness of representation. Without reference to likeness, it possesses feeling because all the feelings in regard to it, are ultimately made on the grounds of feeling.'

obert Motherwell *Cambridge Collage*
échirage: this collage is typical of Motherwell's island
rms; a *papier déchirage* with overlapping areas floating
ove the bank of coulage (leaking point)

Robert Motherwell   *Les Ballets Basque de Biarritz*
Mixed Media: the cloud image areas of oil paint on paper
which form the background are overpasted with a direct
and precisely placed ballet ticket statement—an example
of Motherwell's straightforward brevity

Barbara Engle *In Front of Behind*
Déchirage: suede type of rice paper, matt and soft looking, colour scheme ranging from the palest of greys to blacks, with some yellows near the centre groupings. This is an example of the *déchire* technique, with the subtle groupings of opposing tones creating three-dimensional form floating to and fro in space

BARBARA ENGLE

Barbara Engle Comments: 'I do not start designing with any preconceived idea. I tear and cut many shapes and then start organising them (pushing them around) to fit into my working or design area. This arranging and re-arranging continues until I am satisfied that they are, for me, in the right position. I glue as I go along. If I create more, or different problems as I progress, so much the better. It is more interesting and stimulating than to have everything worked out properly before finally glueing down.'

Ben Norris gives some notes on the development of the mural illustrated:

'The entire project was developed in close collaboration with the architect. Thus the murals were conceived from the outset as part of the basic architectural solution of the problems posed. The 'Gold Screen' sections took on a form related to Chinese or Japanese hand scrolls because of the many columns in the old building which then had to remain in the main banking space. This meant that as spectators moved though the area they saw endlessly variable portions of the screen, but never an uninterrupted whole composition.

'The 'Blue Panel' (not illustrated) is sited in different physical conditions and relates on axis across the entrance and exit axis to an area of blue accumulation in the 'Gold Screen'. The 'Blue Panel' is also interrupted by columns, although in a different rhythmical sequence.

'Thus the origin of the work is a rather well developed sense of architectural space, rhythm and scale—all of this worked out within carefully measured limits. The forms themselves developed very freely in the course of the work. There were no detailed preliminary composition studies submitted in advance, but there was a rather extensive series of 'facsimile' samples prepared which gave information on exact colour, texture and general quality of the surface.

'Because of the time schedule for re-modelling it was necessary to work off-site in order to have everything ready for opening just as soon as the space could be made habitable. A small crew of assistants was hired and an unused chapel rented for a few months. There the 'walls' were built of 3" Masonite on temporary supports. The murals were then carried to completion, after which the new surface was sliced apart at the Masonite joints with a razor blade. The panels were then moved separately and installed on the prepared wall surfaces in the building.

'It was for this job that I developed my own use of acrylic polymer coating over paper collage in order to meet the practical requirements of durability and resistance to soiling. The papers used are all Japanese, mostly hand-made, but all coloured with artist's pigment for this purpose, as the available coloured papers are unreliable as regards to fading, as well as being far too limited in colour range.'

Ben Norris   Mural Panel in Kapiolani Office First National
Bank of Hawaii in Honolulu.
Déchirage: the colouring of this mural is exotically brilliant,
evocative in quality of the strangely beautiful vegetation of
the island. Non-representational, but conveying in its
structural discipline the stark volcanic menaces that lie
beneath

John Kjargaard is a Danish artist, who has lived and worked for the greater part of his life in Honolulu. His work expresses the strong formal qualities that are inherent in the fragile, lacerable Oriental papers that he uses. He makes the following comment on his technical approach to collage:—

'I use the Japanese handmade rag paper, and usually find it necessary to dye a number of sheets in order to get the intermediate shades that I need. They are pasted down with acrylic vinyl copolymer (New Masters) or as an alternative I use flour paste with a few drops of formaldehyde.

Usually I start a collage with a definite idea in mind but without any pre-conceived notion as to what the final result may be. In the case of 'Ah Fong's Garden' the source of inspiration was one of the turn-of-the-century Chinese gardens, of which Honolulu still has a few left.'

I try to avoid 'painting' with the paper, preferring to allow its texture, the torn and cut edges, to give the character to the collage. The colour scheme is black and green, the left side being black with barely discernible shades of blue, grey and green. The right side has greens varying from yellow to almost blue. Finally a touch of ochre brown to break the harmony.'

John Kjargaard   *Ah Fong's Garden*
Déchirage: a fine example of *déchirage* showing the imaginative use of Japanese rag paper. The establishment of three-dimensional space registers in the illustrations

Ah Fong's Garden (detail)

Jay Hannah *China Cove*
Déchirage: an abstract-figurative collage in which tinted
Japanese rice paper is over-laid—one sheet over the other—
toning the colour in much the same way as mixing colours
in paint

Winnifred Hudson *Weather*
Déchirage : 'Weather' may be termed a collaged oil in that
the paper, which is mostly found scrap paper, is applied
over, around and through an oil underpainting, sometimes
being painted over as well. White glue is used as an adhesive

WINNIFRED HUDSON

Winnifred Hudson works on the principle of forming the design elements of a
collage by the building up of laminations of textured Japanese paper in opposition to the flat areas of torn paper. Tissue paper is dyed or tinted by soaking
in a puddle of water colour (artist's colour is used, as poor quality paint tends
to fade). Tints are added as required, and the paper is dried by hanging flat
from pegs or pressing flat against glass. All her paper is processed in this way.

Satish Gujral *Collage 3*
Déchirage: luminous paper and tinfoil combine with the torn and wrinkled paper in this scintillatingly brilliant collage. The power of the forms within this strongly conceived composition refute any suggestion of the theatrical

SATISH GUJRAL

Satish Gujral was born in Delhi in 1925 and is probably the most outstanding Indian artist engaged in collage. His technique is basically papier collé and the paper he uses varies a great deal, often being a luminous tinfoil which creates a poetic and mysterious Eastern aura around his formalistic shapes and figures. Usually it is laid and pasted flat, sometimes cut but often torn. His vision is vividly colourful.

Satish Gujral   *Collage 2*
Déchirage: this collage depends on several media, paint,
paper and newsprint and traditional folk pattern. Both
tearing and cutting techniques are used

Collage I (detail)

Satish Gujral *Collage 1*
Déchirage: the evocative Eastern quality of this collage is in
interesting opposition to the rather formalistic building up
of the composition. Strange relationships to machine forms
emerge in an Oriental aura. The detail shows the media used
and the fusion of tissue paper and paint, and the colour
plate projects its brilliance

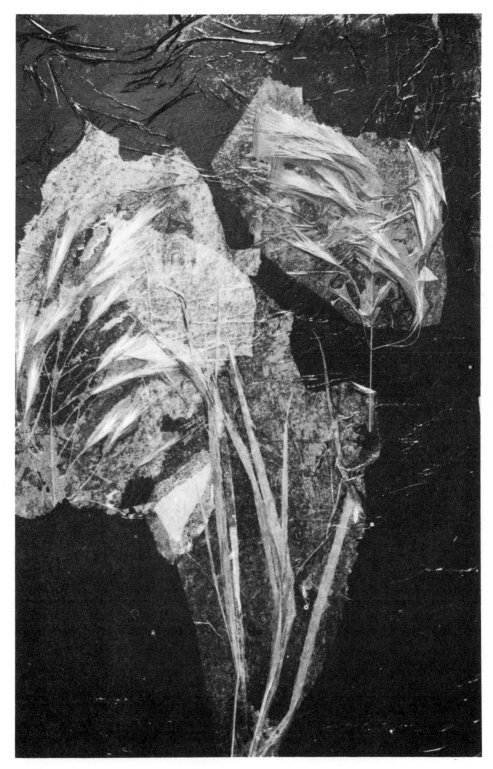

Student Work
Déchirage Mouillé: in this example, dried grasses were placed
on a base of glued black paper which was pressed and ripp-
led while wet with paste. The grasses were overlaid with
white tissue paper, moistened with glue, using several
layers. When dry these layers became transparent and the
form and colour of the grass showed through

65

Student Work
Décollage: in this collage the paper and newsprint has
torn away; the stones and pebbles emerge like i
stations. Several layers of dark toned tissue paper were
in this and all overpasted while wet with a Polycel wall
paste

Décollage

This involves the action of unpeeling or tearing away the paper which has
been previously wetted and glued. In collages of this type, the general
procedure is to colour several sheets of paper (with oil, acrylic, water colour
or ink) and paste them down, layer upon layer, until five or six thicknesses
have been laid.

The peeling down through these laminations (often while still wet)
discloses areas of differing colours or tones which create a sense of three-
dimensional space; forms dissolve into shadows while other shapes float
forwards coherently asserting their presence.

Various ways of doing this present themselves: Layers being torn away
while still moist with glue, give only a limited control of the design; forms
may be deliberately cut out and the unpeeling started at the cut edge, giving
clearly delineated shapes; burning or scorching can disturb a surface, leaving
the texture of a carbonised edge as a reminder of the vulnerability of the
medium.

Froissage

Paper may be wetted or used dry for this type of collage and more usually it is combined with other media. Movement and rhythm are suggested on a static plane by the creasing and ribbing of the paper; breaking the quiescent surface by rumpling, rucking, and wrinkling awakes the inert into a ferment of activity—the expressiveness of paper is infinite.

   The fine Oriental tissues already described are probably the most responsive to this treatment, their fragile transparency allowing unlimited mobility. This paper may be used in several ways. It may be crumpled up before being laid down and then brushed over with a liquid glue while being held in place. It may be laid onto a prepared, glued surface and disturbed as the hand dictates. Sticks, grass, stalks or seeds may be over-pasted with transparent paper which holds them *in situ* while suggesting only vague echoes of their reality on the surface.

   Dubuffet uses crushed leaves, sticks, the dried and flattened skins of fruit and and plants. Burri and Crippa rumple sacking and cloth. Others combine these techniques as an extension of others.

Froissage: a selection of Japanese papers, some torn and creased to show *Froissage* effects possible

Ben Norris   *Penetrated Landscape*
Frottage Collage: prints from a plywood block, used formerly in a woodcut print. Printed in black at random on various hand-made papers. Two or three were sliced up diagonally and assembled with strong colour showing through in the 'X'

Frottage

This indicates the transference of surface forms and patterns, generally in low relief, by rubbing. It is, in fact, the well-known method for taking the familiar brass rubbings, but the imaginative genius of Max Ernst soon projected it along other paths. He became fascinated with the textures and patterns of wood, seeing strange images and symbols emerging from rhythmic forms. Pressing paper against the wood grain, he made rubbings, the prints from which he cut and collaged surrealist montages. Further experiments were made by pressing canvases onto textures, coating the surface with paint, and then scraping it away with a palette knife.

Thin paper is generally used for *frottage* prints, and the cut-out areas of these applied as indefinable units or anonymous sections. Ernst is, of course, the master of this. Actual details of frottage prints are illustrated and a section of it may be seen in Ben Norris's work *Penetrated Landscape*.

Mixed media

As the name implies, this is a combination of two or several media with paper or any collage material, and, in fact, most artists work on the principle of the union of objects and matter, often of disparate origin.

The integration of an idea is often achieved by drawing or painting over the collage after it is apparently completed. John Hultberg's *papier collés* are over-painted with tinted glazes of acrylic colour after his magazine photographs are glued down. He describes his technique very fully on page 75.

Schwitters combined torn and cut paper with innumerable other media: oil paint and fabric, tickets, labels, corrugated cardboard, wood, tattered fragments of dispersion. Considered by many to be the greatest modern master of collage, his 'Merz' assemblages (he refused to call them collages) of old tickets, driftwood, wires, bones, wheel parts, buttons, old lumber from junk heaps and rubbish, were welded into his memorable collages.

Dubuffet, another great master of this art, has united seemingly outrageous combinations of media, as the reproductions will show.

The technique of *Décalcomanie* was based on the Rorschach ink blot theory which was used by psychologists to interpret their patients' unconscious fears and repressions by means of the symbolism represented by the pattern made by the blot. Schoolboys have traditionally dripped ink on paper, folded it, and been amazed and fascinated by the resulting grotesque figures. Ernst explored this further possibility. In place of folded paper he has used two surfaces of canvas with a layer of wet paint in between, peeling them apart to disclose strange patterns, colours and forms.

This technique embraced systems uniting method and accident. The peeling apart revealed weird, fortuitous forms that brought into physical being the world of suggestion that was *décalcomanie*.

No clearly definable example of this technique in its' pure form is reproduced although in several cases it occurs in Mixed Media.

R. B. Kitaj *Glue Words* (right)
Mixed Media: the positive-negative form of
this collage in print reversal, oil painting,
fine drawing is an example of Kitaj's
directness of statement in this vehicle

R. B. Kitaj *The Cultural Value of Fear,
Distrust and Hypochondria*
Mixed Media: this collage with its astringent
social message has been designed in several
media; collaged photographs and prints as
in photomontage, with other sections
disturbed by significant brush strokes. The
work has finally been printed by silk screen
method

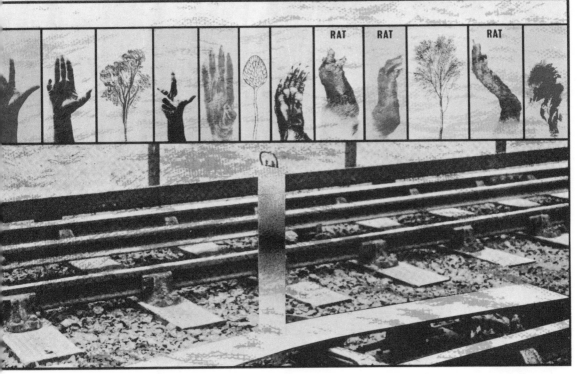

Max Ernst *Mer et Soleil*
Mixed Media: an unusual collage for Ernst with an over-
pasting of formal wallpaper on a thick impasto of oil paint

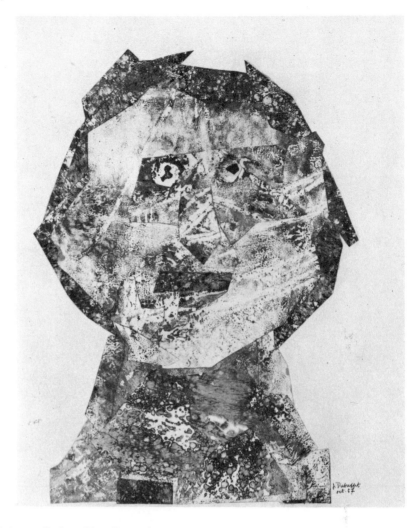

Jean Dubuffet *Peinture d'Assemblage* Portrait
Mixed Media: this *d'assemblage* portrait is a collage of
finely textured sections cut and glued down as a *papier
collé;* a *décalcomanie* portrait presenting one of Dubuffet's
anonymous personages

Kurt Schwitters *Mz 245 Mal Kah*
Mixed Media: a collage influenced in its format by the
volume of poetry 'Anna Blume' written by Schwitters in
1919. The poem, his *Merz* writing was based on the same
principles as his *Merz* painting

John Hultberg *Untitled* (right)
Mixed Media: a very striking example of a Hultberg collage
where the technique of over-painting on a framework of
pictures can be clearly seen. Some areas have disappeared
into a hollow background while others are projected forward

JOHN HULTBERG

'I started making collages about 1950 as a sort of parlour game with my brother, being then influenced by the Surrealists, especially Max Ernst' (writes John Hultberg). 'Along with 'exquisite corpses' and word games they were ways of releasing unconscious ideas that could end up in serious painting. We always worked with photographs and altered them with paint.

'I remember showing a collage to Robert Rauschenberg in 1952. It was done in a technique very close to what I do today except there was less re-touching with paint. He appeared to be enthusiastic about it and perhaps he was influenced by it. I know I was inspired by some of his collages of photographs—I suppose this way of working was in the air.

'About 1959 I made a photo collage which was 8 ft by 8 ft. This was in deep perspective. After this I abandoned the medium until 1963, when I found myself dry as far as painting was concerned. By cutting hundreds of photos out of magazines and arranging them not entirely at random, I was able to make a framework on which to paint, my intention being to change all the forms completely with casein paint.

'Recently I have discovered by accident that instead of pasting down the photos I could print them in reverse by using polymer medium (Liquidex). This is a tricky process in which the ink only of the photograph is left in the emulsion, the paper being peeled away. The ink left is immediately made waterproof by the plastic medium and can be glazed and re-worked, especially as the image is not a perfect transfer and leads to interesting accidents.

John Hultberg *Untitled*
Mixed Media: this collage expresses Hultberg's obsession,
the ruined city of empty houses and broken windows,
deserted squares, watched over by the lonely figure, presented on a grid composition

'I have yet to complete one of these collages, since the process is much
slower and more painstaking than pasting. However I am hopeful that this
technique will be an improvement since the newsprint will no longer be
there to decay. I suppose others have used this transfer method (perhaps with
light-sensitized emulsions) but I have never heard of it and have not yet talked
of it to other artists.

'When I first came out here (to Honolulu) I took up collage again as a
kind of physical therapy. Instead, I went further into it until it absorbed me
completely. The original photos were now wiped out by the paint, showing
only as bases for abstract form. Working with Liquidex acrylics, I found that
glazing the photos lent a richness and refinement—a subjectivity that I was
unable to achieve in oils.'

CONRAD MARCA-RELLI

Marca-Relli became interested in collage during a brief period in Mexico
and has worked in this medium ever since.

Conrad Marca-Relli *Black Rock* (detail)
Mixed Media: Marca-Relli cuts and pastes at
great speed, creating freely and automati-
cally, before the censor of the consciousness
can take over. This collage shows the over-
laying of forms and the dramatic fusing of
the composition. Paint and paper are combined

Conrad Marca-Relli *Octobre*
Fabric Mixed Media: one of the 'seasonal'
collages of Marca-Relli showing a degree of
abstraction created by formal arrangements
of units. The interlocking sections of
canvas are glued down and certain surfaces
disturbed by paint darkened areas

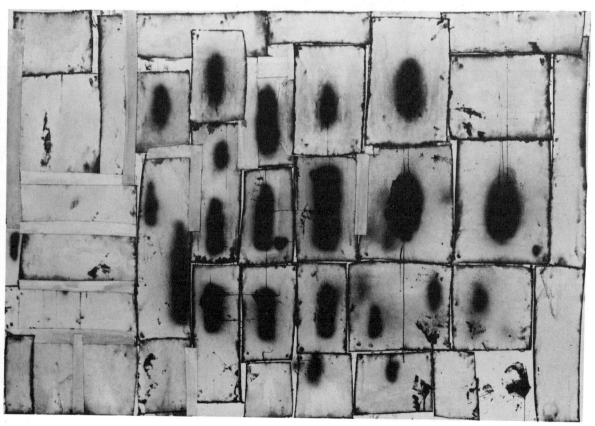

77

Jay Hannah *Sea Cypresses*
Mixed Media: this collage, which is figurative in intention
conveys the translucency of painting in the overlaying of
the thin rice paper

As an abstract-expressionist, he works rapidly with no preconceived design, allowing the cut shapes, when pasted down, to build up in laminations,
often in great thickness. Mis-placed shapes are never peeled off but overlaid
by yet furthur ones. Deep projection and interesting textures result from this
spontaneous approach and the collage retains its original freshness.

In some of his earlier work, amorphic human forms tentatively emerged,
but abstraction has always dominated.

Most of his collages are based on an oil painted canvas base, the paper
form pressed onto the wet paint causing the colour to squeeze out round the
edges giving the effect of an outline drawing.

'Collage is a way to deal with shapes and not get lost in details,' comments Jay Hannah. 'Consequently I find it a much freer medium to work in. It's a way of seeing in terms of shapes. The fact that they can be moved around gives the design a better chance to develop without being forced.

'Sometimes I colour my own paper—newspaper or any other kind of paper that I can get hold of—using oil paint thinned with turpentine. Tissue papers I colour with a light watercolour wash. When the papers dry they are much like ordinary coloured paper but they give me a better 'palette'.

'I use a polyvinyl glue, such as Elmer's ,which is white in colour and dries transparent. I usually thin this glue with water. Recently I have used an even better glue called Gel (made by Permanent Pigments). This glue is more stable in that it does not shrink or expand. This same glue also works with casein paints or acrylics and makes the colour transparent.'

The works reproduced are fairly representative of the feeling that Jay Hannah is talking about. 'Sea Cypress' and 'China Cove' are both pure collage with ink drawing over a gesso base. 'Federal' is abstract in conception with spatial qualities and overtones.

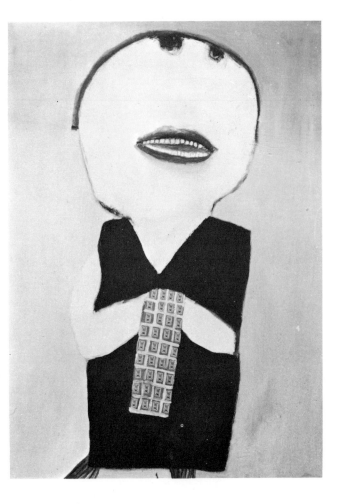

Patricia Douthwaite *Happiness is Green Stamps*
Mixed Media: a combine collage in which the background and the figure are painted in acrylic gloss paint and the stamps are glued on to the centre of the form. A slightly acrid social commentary

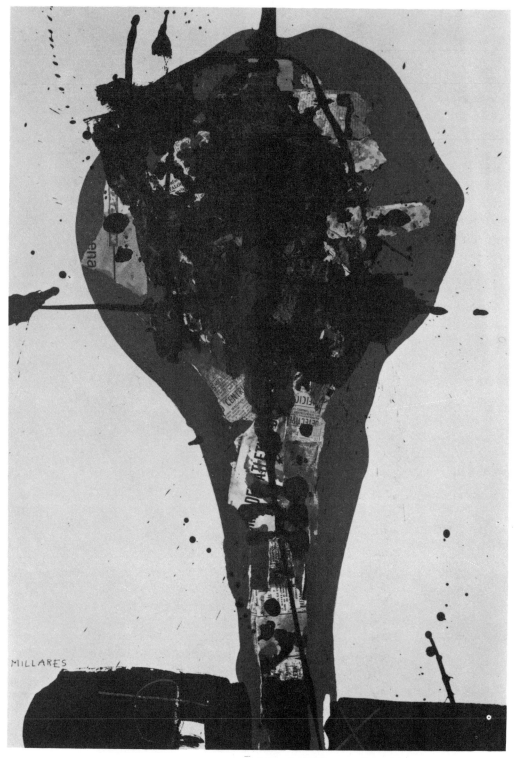

Manolo Millares *Rojo, blanco*
Mixed Media: Paper Collage, with gouache and ink. Millares combines several techniques, using hessian (burlap), old sacking and paint. The example shown in the illustration is based on paper, with torn newspaper pasted on to it; the whole having been worked over with gouache and ink, creating a striking, featureless personage

John Hultberg *Untitled*
Mixed Media: the vivid spatial blues of this collage are the result of over-glazing in thin acrylic paint the pasted down photos from magazines. These formed the framework which may have been considerably altered by the over-painting

R.B.Kitaj *For Fear*
Mixed Media: a discipline of spacing and comment dominates this collage, incorporating several media. The first window 'For Fear' presents the reversal of a negative, followed by a collaged cut-out form, overlaid lines, the head in direct brush strokes, the fragility of the water colour symbol, leading to the photograph of Christ in the garden, the formalized op. patterns and the succulent lozenge forms

May be classified as a photographic surrealist, but he strongly opposed the popular belief that his work is in any sense symbolic and maintained that if one views anything with the object of discovering its meaning, one no longer sees it as an identity.

He has said: 'The mind sees in two different senses. (1) Sees, as with the eyes and (2) sees a question (no eyes)... When people try to find symbolic meanings in what I paint, they are finding a construction. They want something to lean on. That is what I find so infuriating about people who look for —and manage to find—symbols. They want to be comfortable, to have something secure to hang on to, to save themselves from the void.' (A Conversation with René Magritte, by Suzi Gablik, Art International, March 1967).

His haunting imagery illustrates the surrealist principle of the co-existence of irrational elements on a rational plane.

René Magritte *Green Hills*
Surrealistic Collage: in this 'painted' surrealistic collage, the media are fabric, and a musical score cut to the strange forms that rises over the green hills and a few significant brush strokes

ROBERTO CRIPPA

Roberto Crippa uses the medium of collage in its many forms and media, to project his overpowering sense of fatalism; his basic pessimism in man's future. In his use of blackened carbonised wood, cork, sacking, string, cement; materials in their raw state, he has often rejected any attempt at fusion, preferring to establish the human presence in massive, bulky projection but always as an identifiable abstraction.

He has used driftwood, cork, newsprint moulded wet, long slats of wood, barricades overpasted with newspaper; pitted and hammered metal, holed when molten. His colour tends to be stark and sombre and it is only occasionally that he allows a rich deep red to burn through.

oberto Crippa *Personage*
Iixed Media, combined Collage: a totem figure of one of
rippa's 'Personages' in roughly sculptured newsprint and
ood dominates a ground of heavy brush strokes

oberto Crippa *Vol de la Matière* (left)
Iixed Media: a collage of contrasted media where the
onflict between rough dark texture and strong form
gainst a smooth fragile background creates tension and
isquiet

84

Roberto Crippa *Cielo Rosso*
Mixed Media: the sculptured forms in harmonious laminations press down on bulky presences of wood and cork as an
ominous cloud bank over a darkening landscape

berto Crippa *Mon Soleil*
xed Media: the nail-pitted pallisade forms of this collage
mixed media, with the circular sun-form emerging, are
lt over a middle distance of creased and moulded news-
it

Antonio Saura   *Le Boudoir*
Découpage Mixed Media

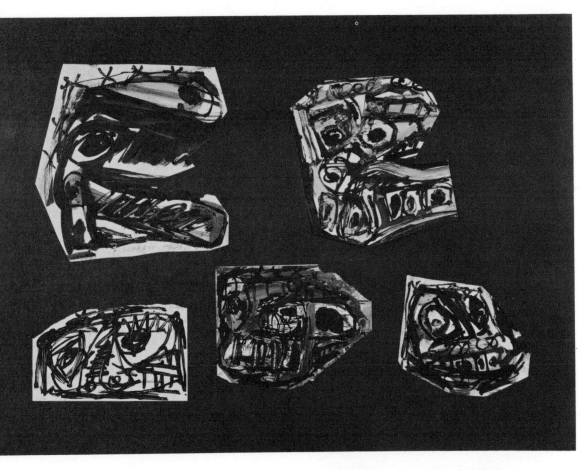

Antonio Saura *Study for Crucifixion 1*
Découpage Mixed Media: ink drawing collage

ANTONIO SAURA

A Spanish artist who has interested himself in a technique that involves *découpage*—the cutting of formal shapes that have been worked on with either gouache or pen and ink, pasted onto a plain background often of striking contrast. Sometimes the calligraphic design is on a base of magazine print or illustration. Two examples are shown here.

Antonio Tapies *Object*
Mixed Media: collage, paper, gouache and string. Tapies'
collages are tenuous topographies of form, using veiled
layers of paper or muslin or threads of fine string suggesting
wrinkled earth. His technique consists in glueing down the
dampened paper on to thin canvas, often ironing it down,
later adding significiant marks. In the first example shown
the paper used is painted thickly in grey gouache and tied
around with string which has also been painted

Antonio Tapies *Collagen No 12 c*
Layers of paper glued on over-painted canvas base

Fabric

Fabric has been used for collage for as many years as paper. In traditional folk art, sections of cloth have been assembled into various design combinations, many taking practical forms, such as the patchwork quilt.

Today the scope of cloth is without limit. The fine silks and brocades of yesterday have been largely superseded by the more forceful and sometimes brutal textures of sacking, sailcloth, worn rags and bandages. Cloth is lined up with paper; fabrics are frayed and shredded and sewn together again.

Burri's bandages and lint, often combining canvas, sacking and vinavil, resolve into his 'wound' collages. Baj uses broken mirror with fine brocades to make up his 'clown' forms in his portrait compositions; a fine balance of the rough and the delicate, rope and silken cords.

The very moving 'Pallisade' collages of Roberto Crippa, an Italian artist, are a fusion of canvas, sacking, string, cork and cement, generally in sultry blacks, smoky greys, browns and white. Nails are used for the eyes in some of the 'Big Heads' and 'Personnages'.

Burnt and smouldered cloth, rigidly bound to a base of cement or glue may be found; frayed or torn or cut into clearly defined incisions.

Mixed media of many kinds, usually joining forces with cloth are found in many of the collages of Schwitters. One illustrated example shows a 'Merz' relief called 'Teeth', where the jawbone of an animal is set on wood and canvas.

Patricia Douthwaite uses discarded paint rags descended from worn muslin napkins, glued into position and overpainted as a sectionally arranged design. She gives some technical details below.

PATRICIA DOUTHWAITE

Patricia Douthwaite comments : 'I started doing collage when I became fed up with the slippery, sliminess of paint... Painting pictures each day and wiping them out each night... I finished with a massive pile of paint rags, mainly muslin baby napkins, covered with beautiful colours...

I began to paint all the wiped-out canvases white again, and ironed out all the paint rags, many of them torn or holed, but laid on the pure white canvas the effect seemed beautiful at the time. I glued them down with transparent glue and painted the remaining white areas with matt blackboard paint.

Jay Hannah *Federal*
Fabric Collage: this is a strongly conceived design using
mixed media which includes cloth and sacking, cardboard
and paint over a canvas base

Patrica Douthwaite working on a Fabric Combine Collage

After this I tore the cloth shapes into smaller sections or cut them into small squares, or tiny match-stick shapes. These were all glued down, line upon line. Initially I had no idea what would result but just played about with the cloth until the bits fell into place...

I next tried using sand mixed with paint, drawing on it with a stick while it was still wet and making sgraffito marks among the bands of cloth... Another experiment was to use cloth stuck down and overpainted, peeling it off when dry *(décollage)*. The imprint of the cloth and the thin thread lines made wonderful map-like textures.

The medium I handle best is undercoated hardboard, surfaced by two finishing coats of Dulux, giving a glossy surface. Whether painting or collaging, I seldom use brushes, except for small bits. I get the best effect by using rags to paint with (the chance effect and not being able to see under the rag until the mark is made, as opposed to the very planned gesture of using a brush.)

The rag pictures appealed to me because the rags themselves were so lovely and so worthless—and there was no need to worry about cost!... Old letters, calenders, bits of shredded curtains, or a piece of browned wall paper... These things are so fragile and useless and sad, but as soon as I have them they become terribly important to me.'

Patricia Douthwaite   *Cotton Collage*
Fabric Collage: in this collage the basic medium is cut strips
from paint rags and hessian (burlap) square sections across
the middle foreground. The remaining background is an
impasto of gloss paint

ENRICO BAJ

Born Milan 1924. Studied at the Brera Academy and at the same time graduated in law.

His interest in the opposition of textures results in the powerful impact of his satirical figures which dominate his collages. Fabrics such as satin and sacking, felt, beading and mirror glass combine on a plane of sardonic humour; the fine and delicate does battle with the coarse and grotesque.

Enrico Baj   *Lady Sensitive to the Weather*
(Winning entry Ascher Award)
Fabric Collage: he has a predilection for materials and with a fine sense of craftsmanship creates a balance between drollery and seriousness

Enrico Baj   *My Love*
Fabric Collage: felt, beading, on a patterned paper b
A sensitive use of fabric material—felt, a bead neck
on a wallpaper base, voicing the astringent comm
from the bits and pieces of the haberdasher

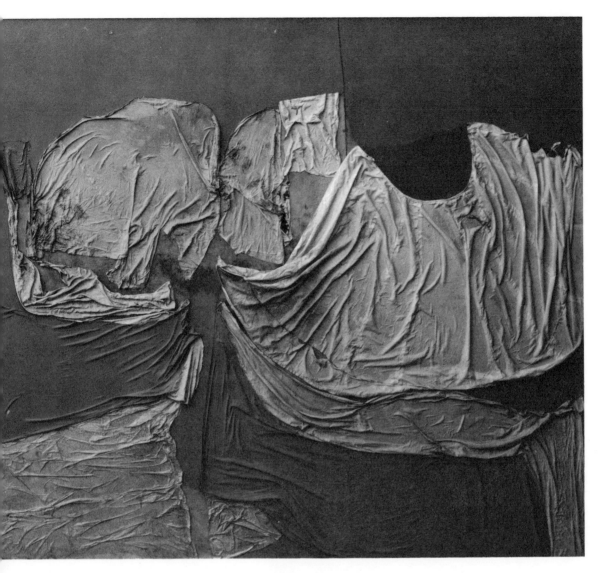

Alberto Burri *Rosso*
Collage in Moulded Plastic: an example of Burri's use of
sheet plastic as a medium to convey the living sensuous
qualities writhing in tormented rhythms

ALBERTO BURRI

The collages of Burri, who is one of the outstanding figures working in this
medium, reflect with great poignancy and strength his obsession with the
'open wound of the world.'

   During World War Two, he served as a surgeon in various field-dressing
stations in North Africa until he was taken prisoner and transferred to a

prisoner-of-war camp in Texas. Here he became preoccupied with art as related to human suffering, and this soon became the overwhelming driving force of his existence. He began by using lint, linen and sacking; the plasticity and spatial movement of his compositions often being heightened by the opposing forces of matt and shiny surfaces, frequently in the same tone. The wear and tear marks on the sacking in some of these early collages, carried forward their original identity and brought a new dimension to his work. In these space designs, strange ruptures are so dominating that one is vividly conscious of the compulsion that runs through his art.

Even in his early works of 1949, these circular shapes appear, often insinuating themselves through from a black background to disclose a hidden dimension. Sometimes the edges swell, crater-like through the torn fabric reminding one of eruptions. Crusts and bark-like tears, red bursting holes become wounded human tissue.

In the wood collages of 1950 to 1959, and in the metal collages of 1958 and later, flames penetrated like lightning into the wood and iron. And in the later plastic collages what appears to be almost an orgy of perforation takes place. 'Combustione legno' (burnt wood) Page 35 shows clearly this technique of burning where the scorched and blackened slats of charred wood form the compositional elements.

Other techniques of Burri's include the stitching together of the tears in sacking and linen, suggestive of the repairing of wounds; the burning of paper which falls, flaming in random shapes onto a prepared background, usually deeply coated with a plastic medium and is later fixed with a liquid of the polymer type. His 'Ferro' (Iron) Page 19 collages are composed of iron or steel sheets, welded under great heat into a rigid assemblage of metallic colour.

The technique of collage is widespread in art today, but the impact of Burri is unique. Werner Haftmann in his essay 'Utopia in Tears' says: 'The sacks of Burri which seek to hide, like torn and dirty dressings, the red of the wound and the black of darkness, express in metaphor the open wound of the world'.

Alberto Burri   *Rosso Plastica*
Collage in Plastic: one of the latest collages done by Burri
in red plastic sheeting, a cauterized wound gapes darkly,
dominating the composition

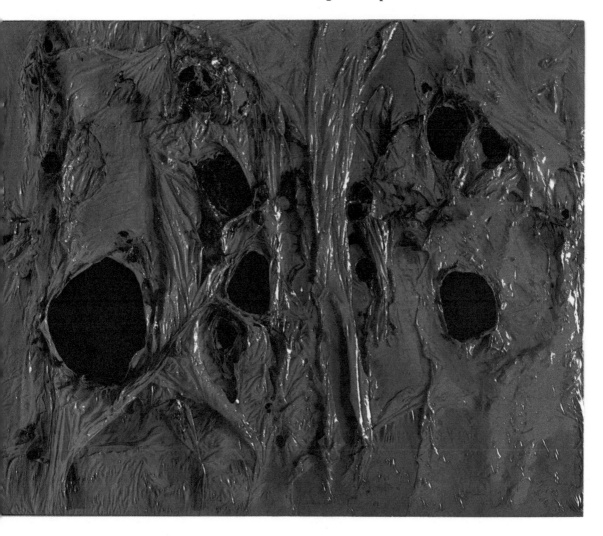

Alberto Burri   *Texas*
Fabric and Mixed Media: this may be considered a fabric
collage as it is used as a basic texture medium in the form of
sacking, torn, worn linen and lint over a pitted base

Combine prints

An accepted method of print-making, this is widely used in collage, being similar to *frottage*. Very interesting techniques have been developed by the Japanese and one known as the 'Combine' print is an outgrowth of the monoprint. The procedure for this is as follows:

Various objects of low relief, such as twigs, netting, sand or soil areas, frayed rope, are glued on to a block or impressed into a cement or plastic medium base. The fabric or paper is applied to this and rolled with an inked

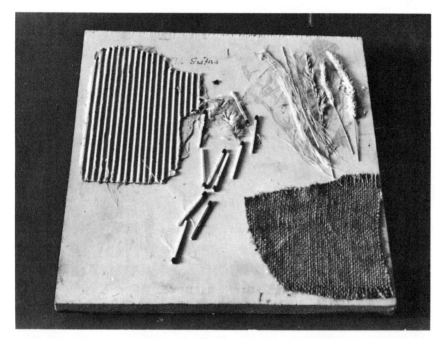

1 Block with elements glued into place (corrugated cardboard, matches, various grass seeds, sacking.)

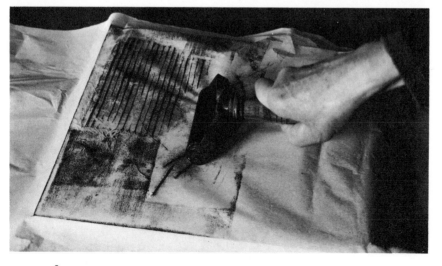

2 The tissue paper laid over the block is being rolled with a printing-inked roller

roller to bring out the textural pattern (low relief is essential or the paper will tear under the stress of rolling). An oil or watercolour medium may be used as an alternative to ink for the printing. (See illustration for details of this technique).

A further method of making a monoprint collage consists in spreading a sheet of glass with the chosen medium (oil, acrylic or printers ink) by means or rolling or spattering. While wet, paper or canvas is placed over this and a pattern design made by 'drawing' with the finger tips or a sharp tool. The paper is peeled off while the medium is still damp and the resulting textured surface left to dry. Other collage material may be laid on this background or it may be cut sectionally.

3   The resulting combine print—a print from a collage

Photograms

This terminology was coined by Moholy-Nagy of the German Bauhaus movement, while Man Ray, who was a pioneer in abstract photography during the Dada period, called his experiments 'Rayograms'.

The technique basically consists in printing such abstract shapes as are created by paper sections or objects on to sensitized paper. Although they may not be regarded as technically collage, the experiments with a machine in the form of a camera brought about an extension of the artist's vision, and this, very often combined with other media, justified the designation.

In the working details of one method that follows, ordinary thin tissue paper is used, torn and set in position on photographic paper, sometimes in several layers, which are re-arranged with each succeeding exposure until the artist is satisfied.

The materials used are as follows:

Photographic paper	A dish of water
A sheet of glass	A timing clock or stop watch
A dish of photographic developer	A red dark-room lamp
A dish of photograph fixer	An ordinary low-powered lamp

The dishes are laid out in this order—developer, water, fixative, on a bench or table in a dark-room, or well blacked-out room. The dark-room lamp should be used in addition to the low-power lamp, which should be in a convenient holder. On the bench are placed the photographic paper, next tissue paper, torn and arranged in position, with a sheet of glass on top to hold it flat. This must be done while the dark-room lamp only is on. Hold an ordinary lamp high over the glass and switch on for a trial period of 5 seconds, using the timing clock for accuracy, and then switch off. The glass is then lifted off the tissue paper and the exposed piece of photographic paper is removed and placed in the dish of developer. The image is developed as far as possible (i.e. as dark), then washed quickly in the water before placing in the dish of fixative for ten minutes.

After fixing, the print is examined carefully in daylight and if the image appears too dark the next one is exposed for a shorter period—say 3 seconds—or alternatively the lamp is held further away. If on the other hand the image is too pale, a longer exposure is made or the lamp held closer. It is important to note that once the correct timing for exposure is found, the light must be held at a constant distance from the paper.

Examples of these photograms are shown here with diagrams. Examples are also shown of the work of Nigel Henderson who has experimented widely in this field.

1 The photographic paper placed on the bench with the tissue paper torn and arranged into position, covered with a sheet of glass to keep flat

2 Trial printing of exposed photogram

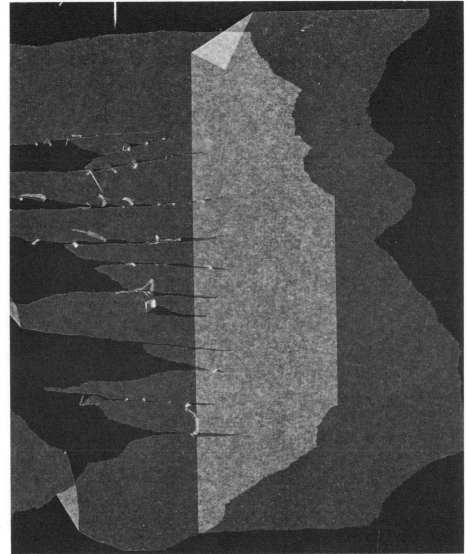

The collage medium in which he works is a combine photo, often a negative and its reversal (positive transparency), bound together and slightly out of register, printed in an enlarger, frequently interfered with by tinting or areas painted out with white or tinted paint. The off-register printing of positive transparencies, features strongly in his collage vision, his purlieu is the decayed element in city plots, yards and streets, his material 'the cracks cantering across walls, stains seeping up like explosions flowering out like pancakes'. He comments further:—

'I thought I would try to write directly to illuminate my work. But I found I couldn't do it. It involved me using words like a critic—in the pretension, for me, of exact word usage. Word—Brick; Wall—Sentence; Room—Paragraph; and the totality of the relationship of house to houses and to environment...

'The calligraphy of Time that reveals, for instance, the sinews, the fibrous quality of wood—the lines of retreat or weakness of materials that reveals its innate quality; as the sand subsides into the water...

'Or as boots broach, their layers arching under uneven strain like geological strata, their leather the rind of fruit, pithy, the cobbler's tacks eager to be out and off, like seed pips...' (Statement in 'Uppercase' 3, 1960).

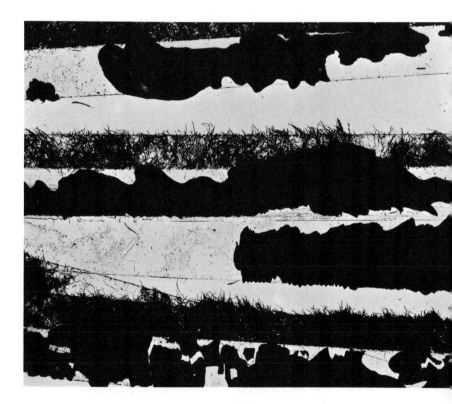

Nigel Henderson   *Small Elements*
Photogram: a negative and its reversal (positive transparency) were bound together slightly out of register and printed in an enlarger. Small nondescript elements were used in the first instance

Nigel Henderson   *Landscape*
Photogram: sellotape (scotch-tape) ripped off a wall where
 had been holding up black paper. Sections of wall distem-
er and hairy fragments of paper. Greatly enlarged by
irect printing through photographic enlarger

Nigel Henderson   *Vegetable Analogy*
Photogram: a garden out of a gardening glove. The disintegrating glove opened out and photographed on contrasting film

Nigel Henderson   *Male and Female*
Photogram: reversed gardening glove in part detail. Interfered with by tinting and painting some areas with white paint

Photomontage

This technique may be defined as the pasting of assembled or cut-out parts of photographs into a montage. Developed from various types of trick photography, it was widely practised by the Dadaists as a means of liberation of ideas and relationships through the juxtapostion of these photographic images.

In practice they glued together a collection of cut-out photographs, often provocative in content and presentation, frequently adding pieces of old letters, newspapers or drawings. These combined tone and form in a new dimension; the intense realism conveyed by the cut-outs having the effect of strongly and sometimes brutally enforcing the message.

Hausmann, a prominent member of Dada and self-styled inventor of 'Photomontage' has stated in his article 'Definition der Foto-montage' (quoted in Dada, by Hans Richter, Thames & Hudson, London 1965): 'Photomontage in its earliest forms was an explosive mixture of different points of view and levels... In the specific case of photomontage, with its contrast of structure and dimension, rough against smooth, aerial photography against close-up, perspective against the flat surface, the utmost flexibility and the most lucid formal dialectics are equally possible'.

Hannah Hoch, who was a close friend of both Schwitters and Hausmann was deeply involved in the Dada movement and contributed many of the collages in this technique, some of which are reproduced in this book. Her work, in common with most other work that was done during this period, was largely subversively political often directed against the disintegrating European monarchies.

A further and interesting development in photomontage is shown in the illustrations of Ronald Stein's photomontage collages which are projections in depth of groups and individual cut-out photographs of figures.

Hannah Hoch *Die Dompteuse*
Photomontage: a typical example of the satirical photomontage of this period. The significantly sharp edges of
roughly-cut photographs merge into the hererogeneous
figure breaking its way into the foreground

Hannah Hoch *Hochfinanz*
Photomontage: a fascinatingly complex
photomontage of a pun

Hannah Hoch *Der Traum seines Lebens*
Photomontage: a bitter-sweet commentary
—the framed boxes creating a space projection to thrust the vision forward

DER TRAUM SEINES LEBENS

Ronald Stein   *Half-self Portrait as a priestling demanding to be measured for dark corners*
Photomontage Relief: a depth of over five inches brings this more intimate commentary forward in strong projection. Its message becomes almost verbal

RONALD STEIN

These are collages in depth, the particular technique here being to people a projecting 'stage area' with photographs backed by a stiffener, some monochromatic and some in vivid colour. The artist's social comment is emphasized by this use of the third dimension.

Ronald Stein
Selected Strangers seeing visions of fugitive moralists
Photomontage Relief: this collage in mixed media is, in
fact, a photomontage in depth; the clearly delineated figures
are cut-outs from pictures and magazines placed in perspective scale on a 'stage' of four and half inches deep

Tray in Victorian Motif
Papier Collé: the influence of Victoriana is obvious although the cut-outs were all from the colour supplements of Sunday papers and the slightly self-conscious comment very twentieth century. The adhesive used is a wallpaper paste and several coats of a polyurethane plastic varnish protect the 'scenery'

Papier collé

he literal meaning of this—the pasting on of paper—is a technique which plies to the majority of the collages in paper reproduced here.

The definition of a work in *papier collé* generally implies small-scale cut-outs sembled into a coherent statement, such as St John Wilson's 'Moscow' or e sectionally designed collages of the students of Hawaii University or of npington College.

Victorian Screen
Papier Collé: this screen was made into a collage of cut-outs
from colour plates in magazines and the strong Eastern in-
influence was probably due to a journey through Thailand.
The nostalgia persists through a strongly designed compositional framework

Max Ernst *Le Monde des Flous*
Collage and Painting on Wood: Another collage in Ernst's
latest idiom. The brilliant primary colouring of tachiste
texture composed in cubist forms, backs the familiar
assemblage which again includes the grills of the pagan
temple (see page 24). Ernst notes besides this his refusal to
live as a tachiste.

Max Ernst *Poster for Dada Exhibition*
Collage Poster: this collage poster by Ernst is a fairly early
example of his work in this medium and is expressive in the
literary sense and striking in its formal arrangement

Colin St John Wilson *Moscow*
Papier Collé : an example of pure *Papier Collé* used in an associative but abstract design. The tickets, labels, maps and fragments of a journey are set in a boldly structural composition—an architectural skeleton designed by an architect

COLIN ST. JOHN WILSON

Colin St. John Wilson is an architect whose work takes him on various journeys abroad, often to places where he is very conscious of the social and political scene around him. He has done several collages, using as a medium the fragments of the passing scene: tickets, entrees to important and unimportant functions, labels, photographs, political and nostalgic, maps, wine labels and travel folders; a comment and a record of a way of life.

Kurt Schwitters   *Alfred H. Schutte* (left)
Papier Collé: in this *papier collé*, the neatly cut components
are only partly stuck down on the white background. The
colour accents are mainly mauve and dark blue

Kurt Schwitters   *Koran 20 øre*
Mixed Media: a collage done during Schwitters' stay at his
house in Malde fjord in Norway. This *papier collé* has a
distinctly Norwegian influence despite the Arabic script

Natural Collage

These photographs present a few instances of what may be termed 'natural collage', where the elements and the passage of time have transmuted man-made structures and surfaces into an artefact.

The encrusted, peeling wall of a house in the East End of London, cracked and probably bomb-blasted, evokes a nostalgic history of a sad, dramatic past. In their formal abstraction, the tones and shapes tell their story within a framework of pure collage.

The tar-blistered walls of the old barn doors contribute a relief element forming a disciplined pattern like a Gwyther Irwin composition in cardboard sections.

Examples reproduced may be considered collages that have occurred from natural causation, weathering, demolition, fire, sun or frost. Others may have an intensity of impact, echoing the force of the agent which brought them into existence.

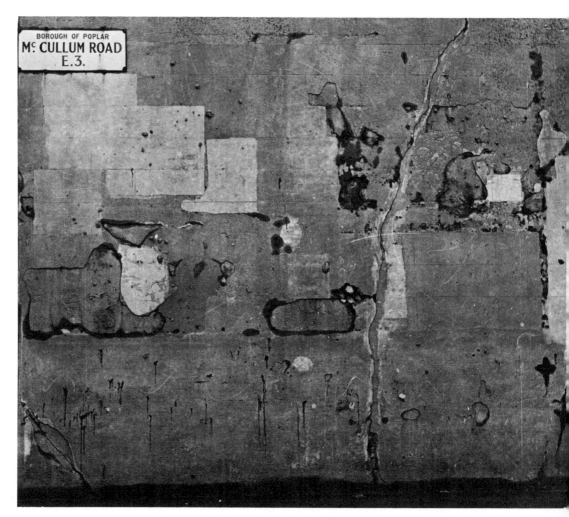

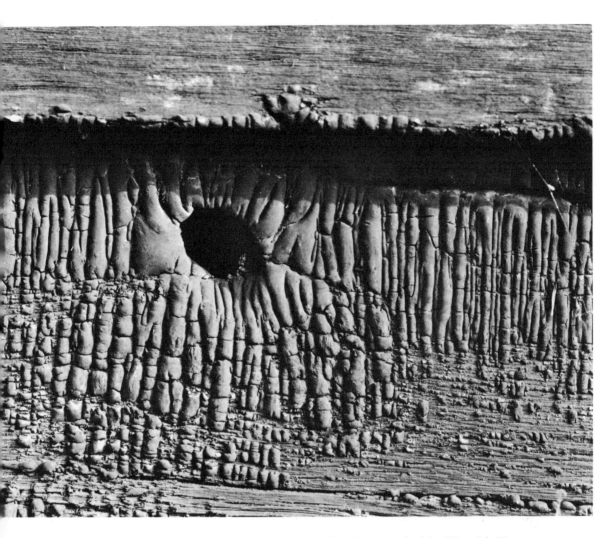

Tarred Oak   Photographed by Warwick Hutton
A further example of erosions, eruptions and volcanic crater caused by the actions of the elements over the centuries

el Henderson   *McCallum Road E 3*
ural Collage: this section of a wall in Bethnal Green,
t London was observed by Nigel Henderson as a pure
mple of natural collage, unselfconsciously embracing
h techniques as *décollage, découpage, affiches lacerés, coulage*
king of paint), *déchirage mouillé, dépouillage* (peeling off),
tage and *papier collé*

Tar and Chain   Photographed by Warwick Hutton
This assemblage of ancient media in the form of rusted
chain hanging lifelessly over the tar-clotted, sun-baked
wood retain their vivid identities in a forceful composition

Part two EXPERIMENTS IN ART SCHOOLS

Working experimentally in the collage medium in art schools has a particular value to students at the most formative period in their lives. In the examples shown, the exercise of composing and re-composing in form, shape and line, undisciplined except for the size of the module is interesting in its approach and resolution.

Impington Village College, Cambridge

Collage on a Theme of Associated Forms, carried out on a Modular Grid, under Ray Malmström, Art Master.

This collage experiment, done by the fourth-year students of Impington Village College on a modular grid idea, carries an association with the Bauhaus School which flourished, in the Germany of the Twenties, under the architect Walter Gropius, who expounded the theory of the modular grid. This same architect designed Impington College in the Thirties.

The pupils of Impington were invited by their master to take part in an experiment to try to discover forms and rhythms which appeared (at least to the pupils) to have some associations with each other. As the size of the work had little relevance, quite small-scale pen and ink designs were decided upon.

Sheets of cartridge paper about 6×7 were damped with water and blobs of black ink dropped on them at random. These blobs spread into various organic shapes which were further developed by additional work with a pen. Imagination and ingenuity both played their part at this stage. Some of the ink forms became flower shapes, insects, rhythmic patterns and spirals. This stage of the experiment intrigued the pupils, both boys and girls, very considerably.

Each pupil was then supplied with a square of paper and on this a rectangular shape ($1 \times 1\frac{1}{2}$) was drawn as a module, and then cut out. Using this frame, the students were asked to select the shapes on the larger paper that seemed to them to be the most interesting and significant; to place the cut-out frame over the chosen shapes and draw a rectangle around them. These rectangles were then cut out and the final part of the experiment embarked on.

1 Ink 'doodles' being explored for design possibilities

2 Module size chosen and cut out of black paper

3 Module frame in foreground laid over drawings. Squaring out of larger sheet seen on right

4 Squared collage backing sheet in foreground. Students adding to drawings in background

5 Laying chosen sections on squared backing sheet

6 Final collage partially glued down

Impington Modular Collage

Pupils were asked to mingle with their class-mates to discuss and then select from the dozens of 'blob drawings' those that seemed to have an association or relationship. Some forms seemed to flow into a unity, others had recognisable image relationships. These were then mounted on to another sheet of ruled paper, measuring approximately 8"×12".

Although the choice of the students in assembling together the 'blob drawings' that they felt had some sort of relationship (however tenuous in some cases) was not always obvious in the finished collage, there was no doubt that the experiment had exercised the imagination, inventiveness, sensitivity and power of choice of the pupils who accepted the project.

A curious feature that emerged during the making of these collages was the intense interest shown by the children in the small 'doodles', which were welcomed as a strange contrast to the usual recommendation to design with large brushes and think in terms of sizeable areas. Moreover, the curiosity excited by the finished collages when they were exhibited was an indication that the experiment had opened up, for them, new fields of exploration in technical approaches.

Photographs were taken while the work was in progress and two reproductions of the final collages are shown here.

Impington Modular Collage

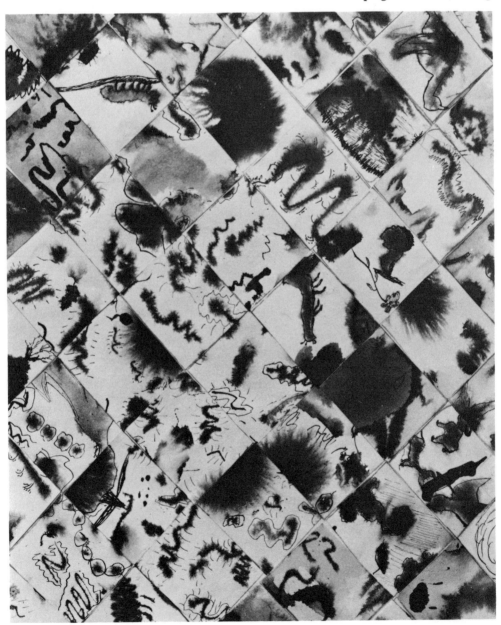

University of Hawaii

Conducted by Helen Gilbert of the University of Hawaii

Helen Gilbert comments:

The class is composed of students who have had little or no previous art training. The problem was assigned after a few weeks of preliminary exercises dealing with two-dimensional construction and spatial ideas in very elementary ways. It was designed to give the student the experience of making what might be called a completed work of art—emphasis throughout is on understanding the creative process as being one in which discipline, intuition and the ability to respond to suggestive stimuli all play their part.

The problem requires some planning and at the same time allows for the development in process of personal vision and an expressive statement which can evolve as working with the material proceeds.

A simple modular grid system is designed which will provide a scaffolding for the final work. The even repetition of the grid system sets up a rigidly ordered field which was enjoyed by some students and used quite obviously in their final work, but which others sought to mask.

At the second stage, students were asked to gather many magazine papers in black, white and grey, or to make a collection of drawings, experimental marks made with various drawing media, or any found paper with handmade marks upon them.

They were then instructed to collage rapidly and freely, tearing or cutting these as they wished and pasting them on to a large sheet of paper. They were asked to be selective only as to the rough tone-value of the collage pieces, so that they eventually made three large sheets which were either basically black, white or grey in dominance. At this point the large sheets were turned over and cut into modules of the previously designed shape and size, with emphasis on precision in the cutting.

It is important for the students to have plenty of modules with which to compose the final work.

The last stage of the job is one in which a good deal of trial and error occurs. Students were asked to experiment with different arrangements of the pieces, moving them in various ways and permitting ideas to emerge which may be suggested to them by the reconstructed images.

They are encouraged to consider the total image which will require a connection and interaction between the various parts. Spatial ideas begin to evolve and can be discussed together with the black and white patterning and textural shifts. The fractured image can become an intensification of reality in some instances, producing the effect of motion of fleeting visual phenomena.

By encouraging an intuitive approach, a good deal of diversification in the final problem will result and students will become curious about the many possibilities that they feel are latent in the material.

The teacher can explore this curiosity by relating the work to any number of ideas about art-making. The rather rigid underlying structure prevents drastic errors in balance, but it may well be too ordered for some.

These students overcame the difficulty by using relatively small-scale units and building a freer overall image (as seen in the case of No 2).

Students tend to exhibit their own subconscious preferences for certain kinds of marks (as can be seen by comparing No 3 with No 4.) The divergent imagery is very apparent.

In the final construction, the repetitive idea of the module can be reinforced by further repetition, (as in No 1 or No 7), or a subtle interweaving of forms can be obtained (as in No 6), which also shows fine tonal quality. In this, the torn edges play as important a part as the grid lines do.

Collage is the preferred medium in the working of this problem as it becomes as creative a means as any other. Its outstanding advantage is the flexibility it permits and the random experimentation it allows. It is a medium which is manageable without too much technical training, and materials are easily obtainable and inexpensive.

The ideas presented here could have been developed into more sophisticated studies relating to colour and three-dimensional constructions.

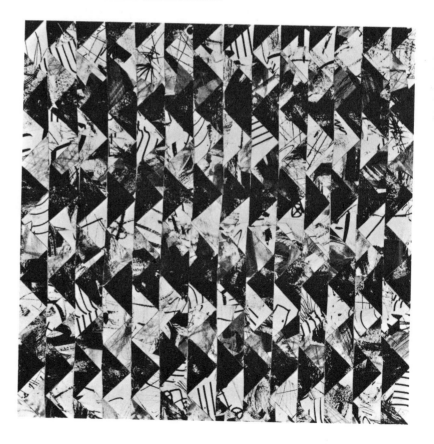

1   Audrey Takaki
Collaged and Inked Paper: the repetitive idea of the module is reinforced by further repetition

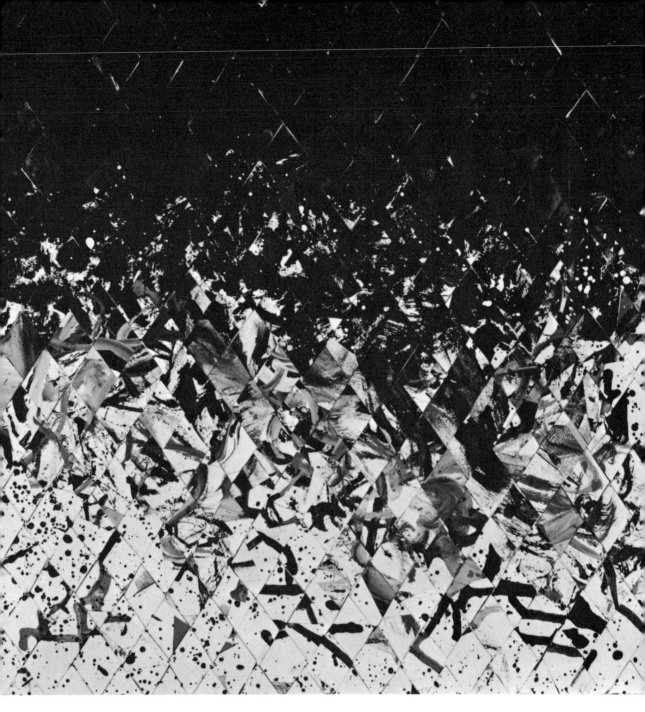

2   Shuron Maradka
Collaged Ink Painting: in this collage, the feeling of ordered
discipline in the rather rigid underlying structure, has been
largely overcome by the use of relatively small-scale units
building a freer overall image

Evelyn Fukuki
[C]ollaged Wash Painting: in this, as in some
[of] the other collages, the divergent imagery
[of] the different students is very apparent

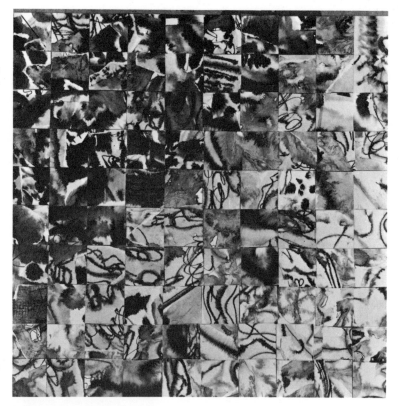

Hovlow Urabe
[C]ollaged Pencil Drawings: strident forms
[m]erge in the imagery of this one

5 Caroline Rho
Collaged Magazine Paper: here where the module is decidedly larger, a striking dichotomy of tone is presented

6 Lynn Yoneda
Collaged Magazine Paper: subtly interwoven tonal forms, combined with the torn edge, play as significant a part as the grid lines

7   Caroline Okasaki
Collaged Magazine Paper: the repetitive framework of the
collage further reinforces the idea of the grid

Suppliers

Papers

Oriental papers, French marbled and many other varieties: T.N. Lawrence & Son, Bleeding Heart Yard, Greville Street, London, E C 1.
Coloured tissue papers, coloured foil papers etc.: Kettles, High Holborn, London W C 1.

Bases

Hardboard, stretched canvas, Masonite, canvas board. For heavier constructions and assemblages: Battened wood, polyester or epoxy resins, concrete, plaster of Paris, gesso
All artist suppliers for canvas board, stretched canvas, gesso, plaster of Paris
Builders' merchants or hardware stores for hardboard, Masonite, wood, plaster of Paris, cement, sand and aggregate
Polyester and epoxy resins: Paint stores, or CIBA: Duxford, Cambridge; Alec Tiranti Ltd, 72 Charlotte Street, London W 1: James Beadel & Co Ltd, Frodsham House, Edwards Lane, Speke, Liverpool

Adhesives

For Paper Flour and water paste, wallpaper paste, Polycell, Casein glues
For Other Media Evostick, Copydex, Bostik, Uhu, Cow Gum (rubber solution)

Paint

Acrylics (Polymers): Cryla from George Rowney, 10/11 Percy Street, London W 1
Polymer from Reeves and Son Ltd, Dept. A, 1 Lincoln Rd, Endfield, Middlesex
Oil paints, Watercolour paints, Coloured inks etc, Gouache, from all artist's colourmen

USA

Papers

Oriental and European papers of all types: Andrews/Nelson/Whitehead, 7 Laight Street, New York, NY 10013-o/s
Oriental papers: Yasutomo & Co, 24 California Street, San Francisco, California, 94111
Mail order catalogues which list a wide range of artists' papers will be shipped to any part of the United States upon request, by: Arthur Brown and Brother, Inc, 2 West 46 Street, New York, NY 10036; and A.I. Friedman, Inc, 25 West 45 Street, New York, NY 10036 ø

Supports

For canvas board, stretched canvas, gesso panels, etc: visit your nearest art supply store

For wood, hardboard, Masonite, and other wood products: try your local lumber yard or building supplier

For Plaster of Paris, cement, sand, and aggregate: available from building suppliers

Polyester, epoxy, and other plastic resins: consult an auto or boat supply dealer, or your nearest plastics supplier

Adhesives

For paper: wallpaper paste, wheat paste, casein glue, and white glue such as Elmer's or Sobo are available at paint, wallpaper, and hardware stores

For other media: contact cement (such as Weldwood), epoxy cement, and white glues are available at hardware stores. Rubber cement, acrylic medium, and sprayable adhesives can be purchased at art materials stores

Paint

Acrylics such as Liquitex, Aqua-tec, New Masters, Hyplar, Shiva, and Politec can be purchased at art materials stores

Oil paints, watercolor paints, colored inks, and gouache are also sold in art materials stores

Glossary

Assemblage   The assembling of different units into collage form.

l'Art Brut   The term applied to Dubuffet's collages in his early exhibition in 1940. Primitively savage work as it existed in early cultures.

Acrylic   Known in U.S.A. as Polymer. A type of paint now widely used by artists, based on the polyester resins.

Brûlage   Burning. In collage refers to paper and rags.

Bauhaus   A group movement started in Germany in 1919, being founded by the architect Walter Gropius. Based on the use of the modular theory, it has had a wide impact on architecture, art and design generally.

Cubism   An art movement that developed rapidly from 1907 until 1925, embracing European art as a whole, although originally it was exclusively Parisian. Breaking away from the Classical vision, it was based on a complete re-orientation of the human image and developed a new system of three-dimensional space relationships. Led by Picasso, others such as Braque, Leger, Severini, Juan Gris became involved.

Combustione Legno   Burnt or scorched wood. A collage technique followed by some Italian artists, notably Burri and Crippa.

Combine Prints   The print taken from a collage made of media in flat relief.

Dada   An art movement flourishing in Europe from 1915-1923, stressing the cult of anti-art. Ernst, Arp, Duchamp, Hoch and Picabia were some of the leading exponents. Neo-Dada later appeared in the U.S.A. with the imaginative experiments of Duchamps and Jean Tinguely's machine of destruction 'Homage to New York'.

Découpage   The cutting and shaping of paper or cloth.

Déchirage   The tearing of paper or other collage material.

Décollage   Unpasting or partial pasting of paper or cloth.

Décalcomanie   The term used in collage for the forms and patterns created fortuitously by pressing together two painted or textured surfaces and then stripping them apart while still wet to reveal a design.

Empreime, Empreinte   To imprint or impress. The print or mould taken by this process.

Elements Botaniques   Dubuffet's terminology for his collages composed of botanical elements, such as dried leaves, grasses, flowers, skins, earth, etc.

Froissage   The crumpling, creasing or bruising of paper or other collage media.

Frottage   Rubbing. To take a contact print of a surface pattern like wood graining by this process.

Fumage   Smoking. The shading or toning of an area by this process.

Ferro, Grande Ferro.   The term used by Burri and others in the contempory Italian movement for their assemblages of welded metal.

Gravure Engraving on any surface to disrupt it or to produce design or texture.

Gesso A plaster of Paris base (gypsum) prepared for use under painting, sculpture or for embedding media.

Gouache Media used for painting and designing composed of opaque colours, ground down and mixed with water and glue. Water is used as a thinning medium.

Impasto The technique of laying on the medium, usually oil paint, very thickly, leaving visible brush or tool marks.

Glazes Colour applied very thinly, usually diluted with oil and turpentine to produce a translucent tone. Often applied on top of another colour to modify the tone and give a lustrous film.

Merz and Merzbild A name coined by Schwitters for his collage assemblages.

Module A standard or unit of size for expressing proportions.

Photograms A method of creating patterns and two-dimensional forms by placing objects or shapes between the light source and a sheet of sensitized paper, and then fixing the image as with a photographic print. Sometimes known as 'photography without a camera'.

Photomontage A technique exploited by the Dada movement, consisting of a collage of cut and pasted photographs, often politically subversive. Surrealism in using this technique produced nostalgic and traumatic collages of dream and nightmare imagery.

Papier Collé A collage of cut and pasted paper, tickets, labels, etc., on a two-dimensional plane.

Rayograms The name coined by Man Ray for his abstract photograms.

Rice Paper The Oriental papers, usually of Japanese origin, used in many collages. A wide collection of textures, designs and colours may be obtained.

Spackle A similar substance to Polyfilla and Sirapite, spackle being used in the U.S.A. for similar purposes—an embedding base for collage media.

Surrealism An art movement following Dada which found expression in the field of literature and art. It attempted to project the subsconcious mind by imagery and dream sequences and associations. The outstanding figures were André Breton *(Manifesto of Surrealism)*, Max Ernst, Salvador Dali, René Magritte, Joan Miró, etc.

Tachiste One who works in the style or technique exploiting the tactile qualities of the medium by means of dripping, or splashing it onto the canvas.

Vinyl A synthetic material similar to the plastic used by Burri in his collages '*plastica*'.

Welding The action of uniting metal, sometimes by hammering but usually by subjecting it to a degree of heat that softens but will not melt it.

The illustrations

Index